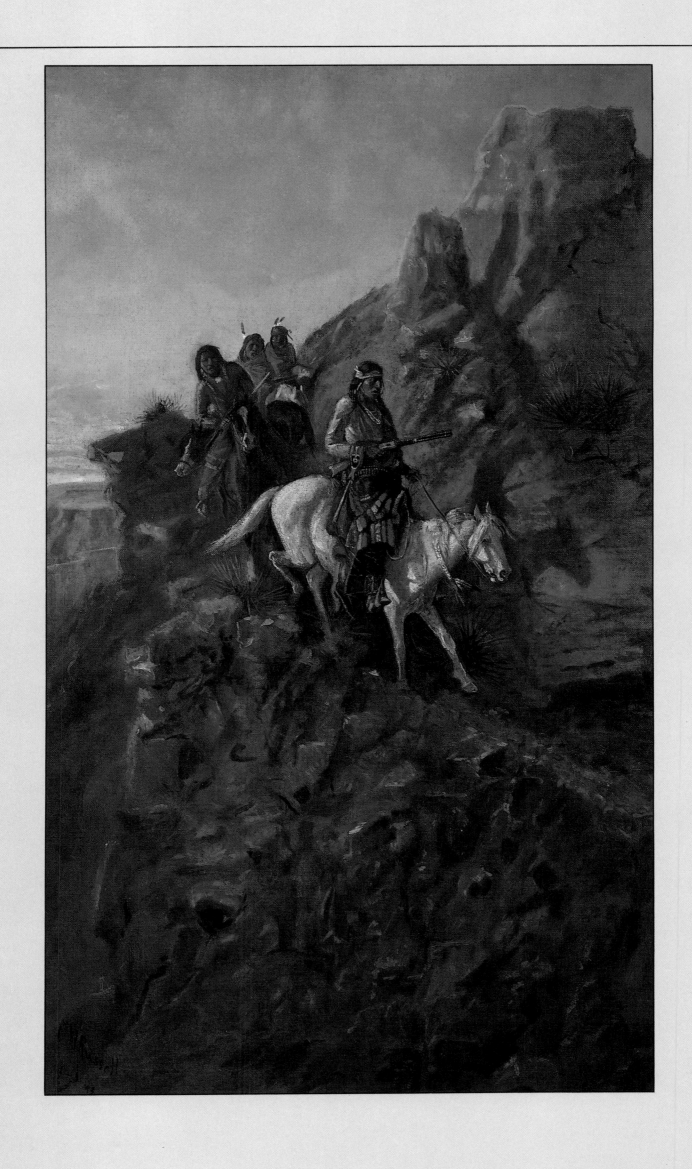

CHARLES RUSSELL

SOPHIA CRAZE

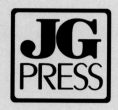

JG
PRESS

Reprinted 2003 by
World Publications Group, Inc.
455 Somerset Avenue
North Dighton, MA 02764
www.wrldpub.com

ISBN 1-57215-352-0

Printed and bound in China by
Leefung-Asco Printers Trading Ltd.

10 9 8 7 6 5

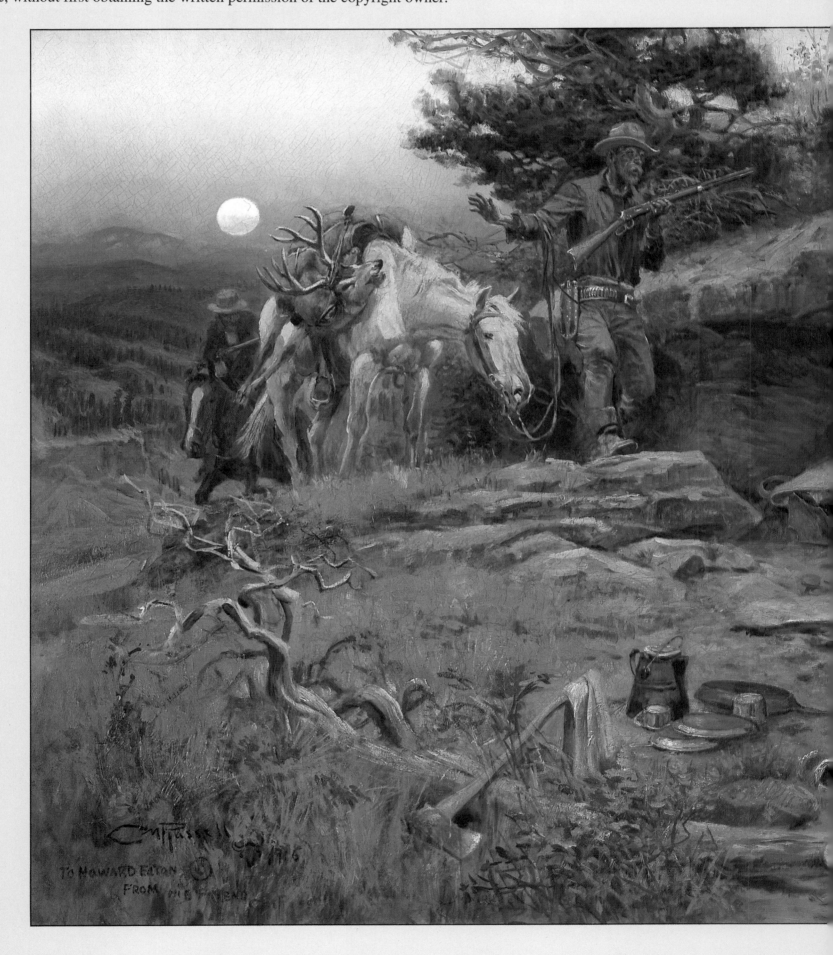

Contents

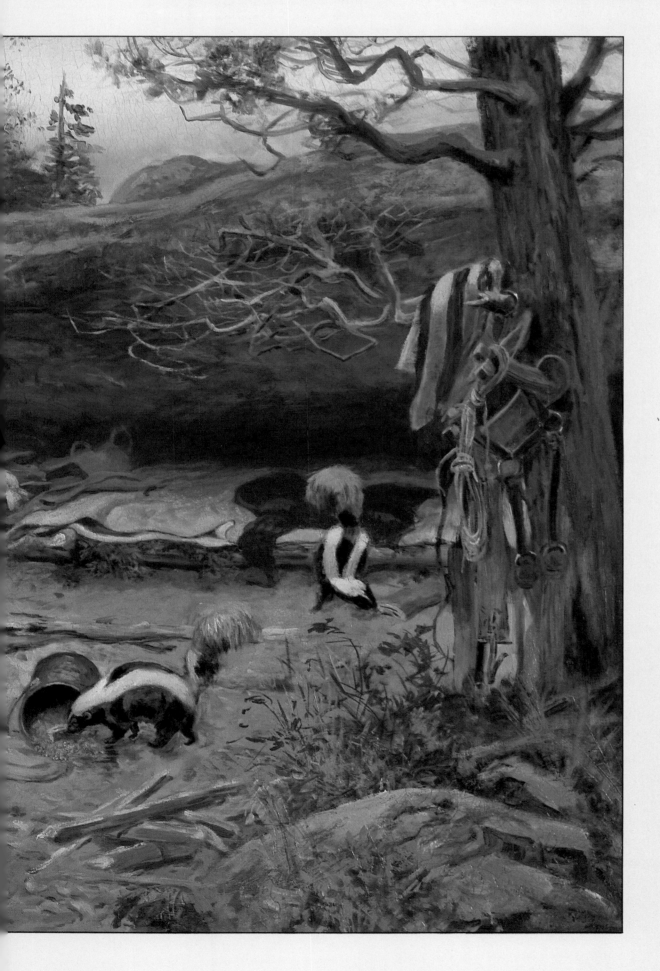

Page 1: C. M. Russell in his log cabin studio in Great Falls, MT, painting **Sacajawea Meeting Her People** (1918).

Page 2:
There May Be Danger Ahead
1893, oil on canvas, 36¼×18¼ in.
Sid Richardson Collection of Western Art, Fort Worth, TX

Pages 3-4:
Man's Weapons Are Useless When Nature Goes Armed
1916, oil on canvas, 17¼×28¼ in.
Sid Richardson Collection of Western Art, Fort Worth, TX

INTRODUCTION

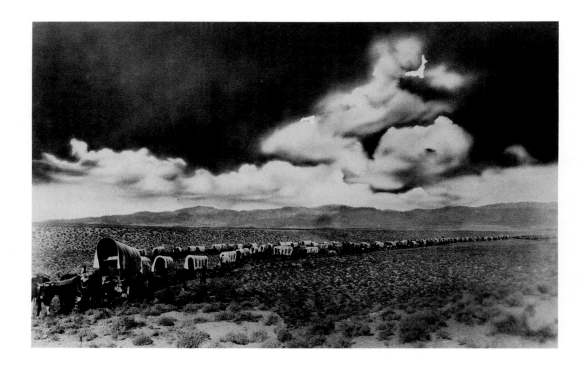

Images of America's last frontier, the Wild West, conjure up the romance of the pioneering spirit upon which the American dream was founded. The West was a world unto itself, peopled by such colorful figures as Buffalo Bill, Will Rogers, Kit Carson, George Custer, Chief Joseph of the Nez Percé Nation and Sitting Bull of the Sioux. It was also a changing world in which countless farmers, cowboys, soldiers and prospectors gradually took over territories formerly occupied by such American Indian tribes as the Crow, Flathead, Piegan and Blackfoot.

Into this world rode Charlie Russell in a stagecoach when he was 16 years old. Since he was a small child, Charlie ached to go west. Finally, his father sent him on a visit to Montana in the hope that his son would satisfy his youthful craving for western adventure and then settle down to serious responsibilities of life. On the contrary, young Charlie's infatuation for the West developed into a deep attachment; his first trip there extended into a lifetime, forty-six years. Charlie instantly felt more at home in Helena, Montana, than he had ever felt in St. Louis, Missouri, and he resolved to stay.

After a short and unsuccessful stint as a sheep herder, Charlie worked as a cowboy for eleven years. During these years, he eagerly sketched, painted and sculpted the wonders of the West as he experienced them – the grueling life of herding cattle on the range, the customs and rituals of various Indian tribes, the array of wild animals roaming the scorched grass of the plains, the wild and woolly recreation of cowboys shooting up towns. Appropriately, Charlie became known as the "cowboy artist" as he authentically reproduced the rugged West as it once was.

Charles Marion Russell was born to Mary Elizabeth Mead and Charles Silas Russell on March 19, 1864 in Oak Hill, Missouri. Charlie was the second son of six children, one girl and five boys. For generations the Russell family line produced prominent members of society. Charlie's great-grandfather, Silas Bent, was a chief surveyor of Louisiana Territory and later chief justice of the supreme court of Missouri Territory. Charlie's great-uncles were pioneer fur trappers, the best-known of whom, William Bent, built the first trading post on the Arkansas River in 1832. Charlie's father, a graduate of Yale, owned large tracts of land and helped manage the family-owned mining business. Charlie's maternal ancestors included "Rifle Jack" Acker, a revolutionary war hero. The Russells expected Charlie to live up to this distinguished legacy by attaining a proper education and assuming a position in the family business.

However, Charlie also inherited the adventuresome, pioneering spirit of his forebears. He became a zealot for the West. From an early age his interest was fueled by ubiquitous western stories and myths. At home, accounts of the daring exploits of his relatives stirred his imagination. Charlie also relished the stories his mother read aloud to him, tales of legendary characters such as Davy Crockett, Daniel Boone and Kit Carson. Moreover, the newspapers of the day were filled with reports of the ongoing Indian wars. Charlie adapted these stories to his own bushwacking games, such as "trappers and Indians" in the woods and romping through the neighborhood cowboy style on his pony.

Much to his parents' chagrin, little Charlie showed no interest in schoolwork. His mother's efforts, and those of an Episcopal priest, to tutor the restless boy were of no avail. If Charlie wasn't cavorting around as a cowboy, he had another outlet for

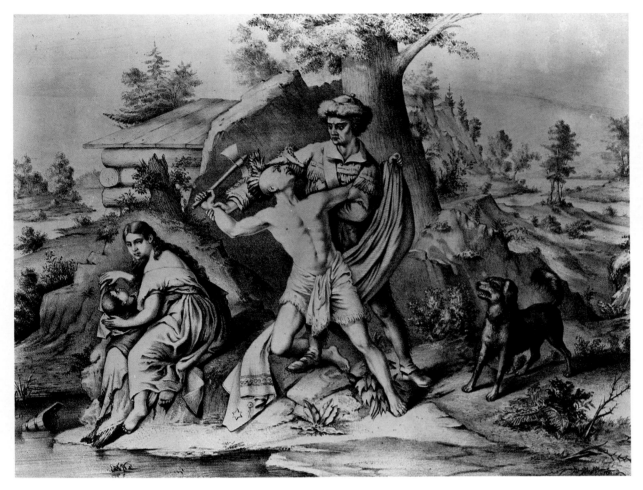

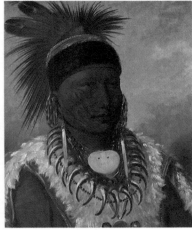

Opposite: Settlers made the tedious trek across the rugged Great Plains in canvas-covered wagons pulled by oxen.

Above: *White Cloud*, by George Catlin (1796-1872).

Left: The romantic figure of Daniel Boone (1734-1820), the daring woodsman and pioneer, protecting his family.

his fertile imagination: drawing and modeling.

Since he was a toddler Charlie exhibited an artistic aptitude. When his mother read the Bible aloud to the family, three-year-old Charlie would spontaneously draw the biblical characters as he pictured them. According to family records, Charlie's first sculpture was of a bear, which he modeled from the caked mud on his shoes when he was four. He soon found more malleable material from his sister's art supplies and later his own supply of beeswax which his parents bought for him. Thereafter, he often carried the beeswax in his pocket, modeling at will any character or animal that came to mind.

Initially, his parents regarded Charlie's artistic hobbies as much a waste of time as his western obsession. However, as his talent became more and more apparent, they grew supportive. They beamed with pride when Charlie won a blue ribbon for one of his drawings in the St. Louis County fair when he was 12. And although they never gave Charlie any formal art instruction, they took him to exhibits of work by such western artists as George Catlin, Karl Bodmer and Alfred Jacob Miller. In the 1830s such artists had passed through St. Louis, then the gateway to the Far West, and their work was popularly exhibited in the area. Charlie was particularly impressed by the native St. Louis artist, Charles Wimar, who had died just two years before Charlie was born.

When Charlie entered adolescence, he continued to shun his school lessons. He consistently earned poor grades in school and played hooky. He preferred to while away a day, hanging around the St. Louis riverfront and its saloons, listening to swaggering cattlemen, gamblers and the like, spin yarns about the Wild West. He also immersed himself in the popular western dime novels by Bret Harte, Owen Wister and others.

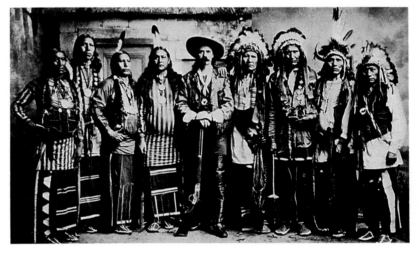

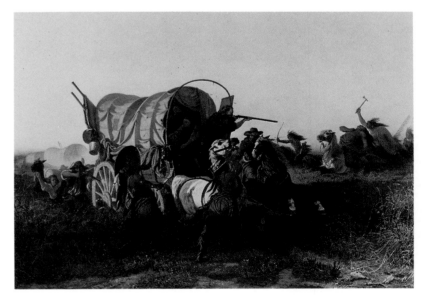

Middle: Founder of Cody, WY, William F. Cody (Buffalo Bill) with Pawnee, Crow and Sioux scouts in 1875.

Above: *The Attack on an Emigrant Train* by Charles Wimar (1828-1862). (*The University of Michigan Museum of Art, Ann Arbor, MI*)

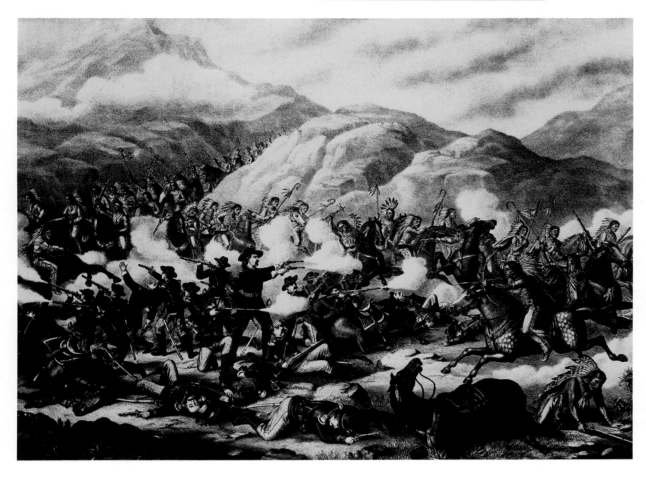

Left: One of the many idealized renderings, depicting "Custer's Last Stand" of June 25, 1876.

Below: Painting of Chief Joseph, leader of the Nez Percé Nation, by E. A. Burbank.

Opposite left: An Arapaho, sitting before his buffalo skin teepee. Such teepees of the western plains were sewn with buckskin thongs and closed in front with wooden pegs; the open flaps at the top – adjusted by poles according to wind direction – served to ventilate the teepee.

Opposite right: By the late 1800s, bison were near extinct, as hunters slew them for their hides. Bison had been vital to the subsistence of the plains Indians for centuries.

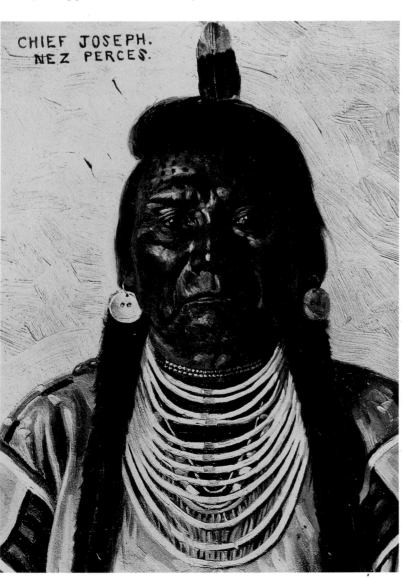

When Charlie was 15, his parents packed him off to a military school far from the West – in Burlington, New Jersey. They hoped that the discipline of such an environment would make their son more studious and productive. But they were sorely disappointed; Charlie spent much of his classroom time sketching cowboys and Indians in his textbooks and the rest of the time "walking guard duty" as punishment for unruly behavior. He left after one term, the last he would ever spend in a formal educational institution.

In figuring out a way to cure Charlie of his mania for the West, Mr. Russell decided to give his son some of his own medicine by sending him for a visit in the West. He thought that the crude conditions of life on the frontier would bring Charlie to his senses. "Since you are determined to go," his father concluded, "it is better that you go in the right way." He made arrangements for Charlie to accompany a family friend, Pike Miller, to Pike's sheep ranch on the upper Judith River in Central Montana. Charlie could not believe his luck and eagerly took off to the land of his dreams.

Although Charlie had heard much about the West, he could not have imagined all that he would encounter on this western passage. The Montana Territory in those days was rugged and remote. Charlie and Pike rode part way by the Utah and Northern Railroad; this was the one existing narrow-gauge railway in Montana, and only a few months before, was built as far as the southern boundary of the territory. Charlie and Pike then took a stagecoach and later a wagon with saddle horses; the tedious trek lasted nearly a month. Later Charlie loved to reminisce about his first impressions of the West, which were mixed:

> I remember when we pulled into a small station near Fort Hall, the platform was alive with Injuns dressed in all sorts of clothes, from a clout an' leggin's to a trader's blanket. I sure was excited; an when we were about to leave, every last one of 'em piled on to the train. Right then I didn't feel none too comfortable.

In the West at that time, the major Indian wars of the nineteenth century had run its course; nonetheless, "white men"

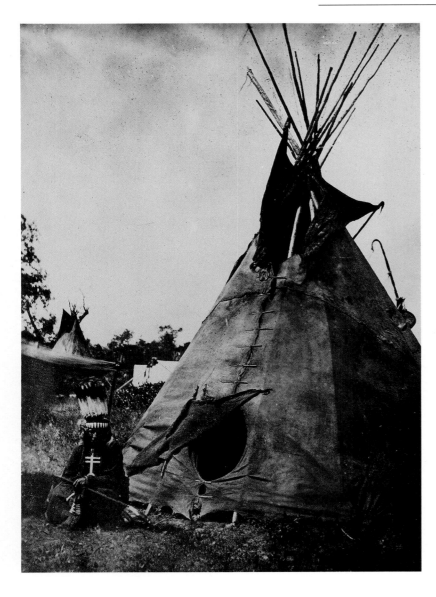

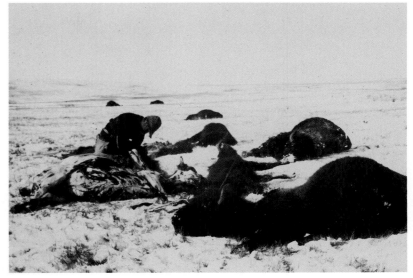

and "red men" were still wary of one another. Custer and his Seventh Cavalry had stood their "Last Stand" at the Little Big Horn River four years earlier, and the last of the Indian battles ended with the defeat of Chief Joseph and the Nez Percé Nation only three years before in 1877. The memories of these bloody skirmishes were still fresh in people's minds. Remnant forts that were built to fend off the Indians, stood as symbols of the racial enmity.

Settlements were widely scattered across Montana Territory. The largest of these pockets of "civilization" was Helena, a goldmining camp with a rowdy population of about 4000 – including cowboys, Indians, miners, saloon keepers, dancing girls, a few bankers, storeowners and others. It was here that the stagecoach leg of Charlie's journey ended. In expecting to see the western storybook characters of an earlier period, Charlie met with some disappointment:

> When I got to Helena, the town was brimful of Flathead Injuns. They'd jes' been paid a lot of money by the government; an' they was whippin' their ponies up an' down the street in bunches. But I was sure disappointed right there. 'Course I didn't say nothin' to nobody 'bout it, but I'd expected to see them Injuns wearin' war-bonnets and all the white men wearin' long hair an' buckskin shirts.

Nevertheless, the real West, Russell began to realize, was far more wondrous than any book he had ever read or anything he had ever imagined. During the few days stop in Helena, Pike purchased a four-horse team, a wagon, and supplies for the last

two hundred miles of their journey. On this last stretch on horseback, Charlie got a taste of some "Injun" excitement.

The "Indian country" was a vast area north of the Marias and Missouri rivers where the Blackfoot Nation and their allies lived. The Crows lived in another large area south of the Yellowstone River. These reservations were for the purpose of confining the Indians, but travelers crossing Montana Territory still feared attacks by hostile Indian renegades.

One day, while Charlie and Pike were traversing Indian country, Russell was riding ahead of the wagon, daydreaming of the Indians he wanted to meet; suddenly he spotted a band of Crows, fully adorned with feathers and war paint, closing in on him. It turned out that the Crows were friendly. They just wanted to warn Russell about the threat of an attack by their enemies the Piegans, who were at large. This experience was the first of many positive exchanges with Indians that Russell would encounter.

After they finally reached Pike's sheep ranch in the Judith Basin, Charlie was given the task of herding sheep. The locals considered Kid Russell, as they called him, an uncouth sixteen-year-old who – in his disregard for the conventions of society – ignored such details as personal hygiene and ran around with shaggy hair, dirty clothes and the like. Regarding his first job, Kid Russell said: "I did not stay long as the sheep and I did not get along well, but I do not think my employer missed me much, as I was considered pretty ornery."

Nevertheless, Charlie was entranced by the beauty of the land and the abundance of wildlife. In some areas the hills were still "black with buffalo," but by 1885 hide-hunters had slaughtered all but a few herds between the Missouri and Yellowstone rivers. Describing the South Fork of Judith, Charlie wrote:

> Shut off from the outside world it was a hunter's paradise bounded by walls of mountains and containing miles of grassy open spaces . . . swarming with deer, elk, mountain sheep, and bear, besides beaver and other small fur-bearing animals.

With his keen observation and knack for storytelling, Russell extensively wrote about and painted the purity of nature around him in vivid detail. Even the leathery, hardbitten locals admired and respected his talent. Entirely self-taught, he perse-

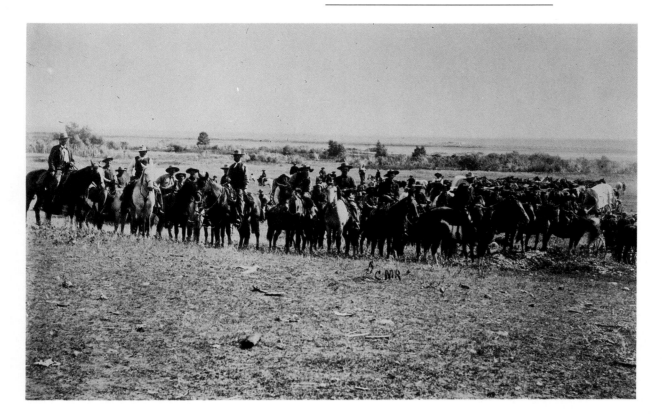

Below: *The Quest* (c.1902), an oil painting by Frederic Remington (1861-1909). (*The Anschutz Collection, Denver, CO*)

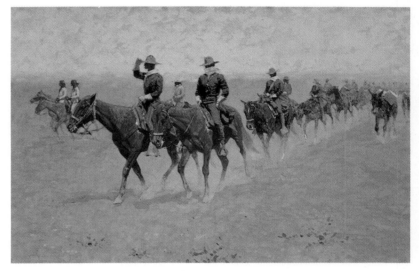

vered at his craft continuously. God, as he said, gave him his talent, and nature was his teacher. Wherever he went, Charlie would delve into his box of art supplies, which contained some small paint brushes, watercolors, a black crayon, and a ball of beeswax. He painted on anything he could find – on the back of envelopes, on birch bark, buckskin, or cardboard. In those days Charlie didn't think of himself as a professional artist and worked solely for pleasure. He usually gave his sketches and models to anyone who enjoyed them.

Russell must have been influenced to some degree by his contemporary Frederic Remington. Both artists had in common a passion for the West and an ability to capture it in mood and detail. Their names were often linked together; but the two never actually met. Russell first knew of Remington through popular magazines of the day, in which Remington's work began to appear in the early 1880s. Whatever inspiration Russell may have drawn from Remington would have been from his common subject matter rather than style, since Remington was primarily a pen-and-ink illustrator in those days, whereas Russell was a painter early in his career.

After his unsuccessful stint as a sheep herder, Russell said that he "took up with a hunter and trapper named Jake Hoover. This life suited me. We had six horses, a saddle apiece, and pack animals." He ended his time with Hoover after two years when he returned to St. Louis to visit his parents. Although the Russells tried to persuade their son to stay, the civilized life in St. Louis quickly compelled Charlie to escape back to the raw country in Montana.

Upon his return, Russell had only a few pennies to his name; fortunately, just outside Billings, he ran into a "cow outfit" which hired him as a night hawk to guard the cowboys' horses at night. The difficulties of such a lowly position included having to endure long hours in the saddle, sometimes in chilling rain or sleet, and chasing after runaway horses.

In being a night hawk "I was sorta shaky at first," admitted Russell, "with so many hosses in the cavvy, but I knowed if I wanted to stick with the roundup an' be a cowhand, I'd have to make a good showin'. I'll say I held them hosses tight – I wanted that job . . ."

After only a month on the cattle trail, Russell and his team joined up what was known as the Judith roundup. In Montana at the time this roundup used the largest cattle outfit – with 75 riders and 400 horses. This was a daunting prospect for a young greenhorn like Charlie; nevertheless, he was given a position as a night herder. In tending the restless cattle at night, Russell had to deal with inclement weather and the constant threat of a stampede.

That fall his team drove one of the largest herds from central Montana to Miles City, where the cattle were to have been shipped east via the Northern Pacific Railroad. However, upon arrival, the cowhands discovered that the construction of this railroad was behind schedule and was not yet laid that far west. Consequently, they were forced to travel another cumbersome 125 miles to Glendive for the train connection.

Charlie's experiences on this two-month cattle drive made a lasting influence on him. In addition to making many friends, he had the opportunity to experience some real "Injun" ex-

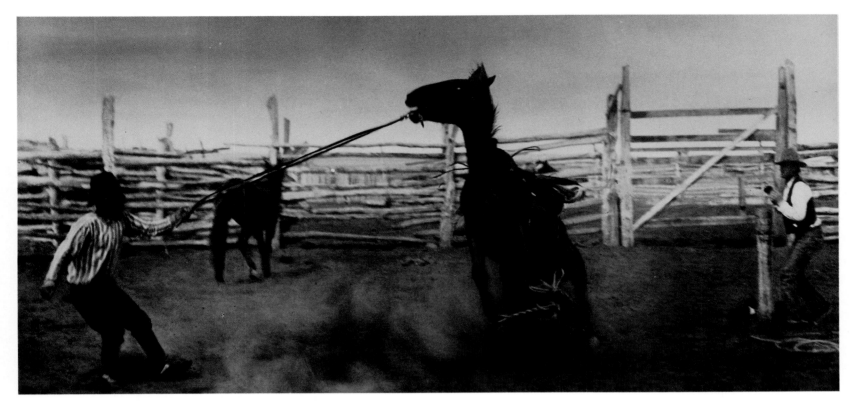

Above: This photo by L.A. Huffman shows how a "cross-hobbled" broncho was broken-in for saddling – by tying together its front legs and a front leg with a back leg.

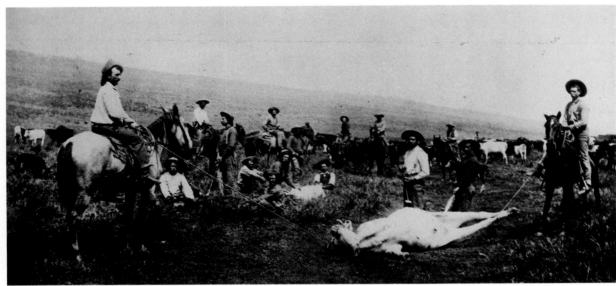

Left: After roping a steer, cowhands branded it with a hot iron of the owner's insignia for identification.

citement. One time he witnessed the aftermath of a battle between the Crows and the Piegans. In addition, he and his cow outfit once fell into conflict with some Indians who demanded that they pay a dollar per head of cattle for moving their herd through tribal territory. When the trail boss refused to honor this custom of "taking toll," the Indians tried to stampede the herd. Such scenes, in addition to the constant daily activities around the cattle camp – provided Charlie with a wealth of material which he incorporated in his paintings and sculptures.

By 1885 Russell began to pursue painting in oils, thereby broadening his palette of watercolors. For months at a time, he went off to Jake Hoover's cabin to paint intensively. Following this period of serious experimentation, Russell captured more effectively, with deeper colors, the glories of Montana – the dramatic rose and gold of sunset and the soft greys of dawn, the ochre and browns of scorched grass, the roaming wild animals, and the Indians and settlers of the plains.

The year 1886 was a devastating one for the cattle industry in Montana. After a summer seized with drought and grass fires, one of the worst winters blasted the territory with arctic blizzards. Stock raisers desperately hoped that a chinook – a warm wind from the Northeast – would melt the snow in time to save their starving cattle.

At the time Charlie was tending a herd owned by Kaufman and Stadler. When Kaufman sent a letter inquiring about the condition of his cattle, Charlie and his partner did not have the heart to tell him. Instead, Charlie made a small, crude sketch – entitled "Waiting for a Chinook" – which pictured an emaciated steer, branded with the owners' "R" insignia, about to keel over in the presence of hungry coyotes. This sketch, later subtitled "Last of the 5000," became famous in the Helena area. It describes more than a thousand words the disastrous winter of 1886 and its consequences on Kaufman's 5000 head of cattle, and many other herds.

"Waiting for a Chinook" hastened Charlie's reputation as a local artist. The *Helena Weekly Herald* noted that Russell's pictures, which had "evolved amid the rough surroundings of a cattle ranch, adorned the offices and homes of wealthy citizens of Montana's principal cities." At this time, *The Independent*, made the first reference to Charlie as the "cowboy artist."

Russell's pictures – the ones he did not give away – were often sold in saloons. In those days saloons functioned as the

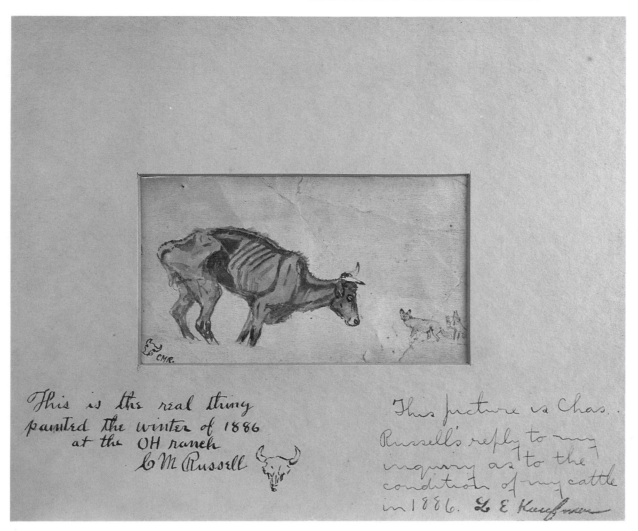

This is the real thing painted the winter of 1886 at the OH ranch

C M Russell

This picture is Chas. Russell's reply to my inquiry as to the condition of my cattle in 1886. L E Kaufman

Left: "Waiting for A Chinook," a watercolor sketch only 3×4¼ inches, documents the effects of the disastrous winter of 1886 on Montana livestock.

Opposite left: Arapaho women performing the Ghost Shirt Dance. After Russell's stay with the Canadian Bloods, he visited the reservations of other tribes, including the Arapaho, and participated in their rituals.

Below: Dressed in authentic Indian garb, with his aquiline features and stoic manner, Russell made a convincing Indian.

Opposite right: Pictured are Nancy Russell (far right) and Charlie, flanked by his nephew Austin and friends, Mr. and Mrs. "Skookum" Hume.

social center of each settlement, the local watering hole so to speak. The saloonkeeper was usually a solid citizen who often served as a lawyer and banker as well; many a saloonkeeper helped Charlie negotiate better prices for the paintings he sold over a drink. He received his first formal commission from a saloonkeeper in Utica who wanted a painting to hang behind his bar. Without canvas or art supplies Charlie made do with a large slab of wood and whatever paint he could find.

Charlie spent the summer of 1888 in Canada. As he and a companion were heading back across the Blood reserve, trying to reach Montana before winter, they met up with some Bloods. It turned out that the chief, Black Eagle, was an old friend of Russell's. His companion continued on, while Russell ended up in the "lodge of his red brothers," for six months until the snows melted in March and the Benton trail opened up. Russell's time with the Bloods deeply affected him; he gained a true understanding and reverent appreciation for Indian life and philosophy.

After Charlie left the Bloods, he was still penniless. As he rode back to Montana upon his faithful horse Monte, ill-equipped to live off the land, he happened upon a long train of overland freight wagons, which gave him a lift. Such freight wagon trains transported valuable furs, foodstuffs and other supplies. This experience influenced Charlie's painting *The Jerkline* which details the jerk-line rein of the wagon train, running from the lead horse's bit back along the line of horses to the jerk-line man who steered the whole string.

In the fall of 1891 Russell went to the World's Fair in Chicago and then back to St. Louis, where he paid a visit to William

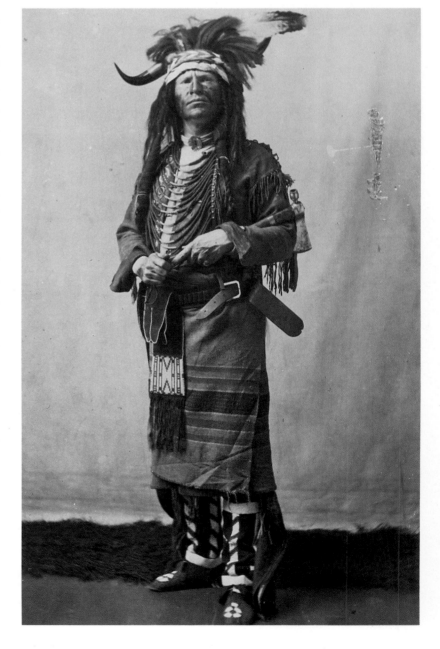

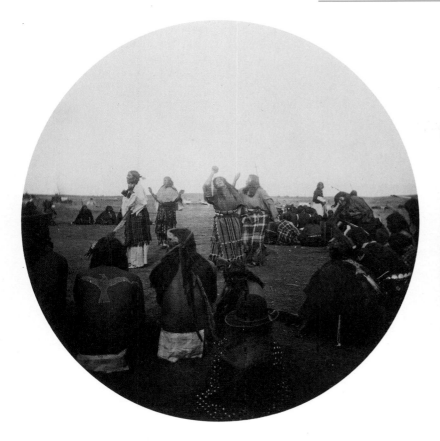

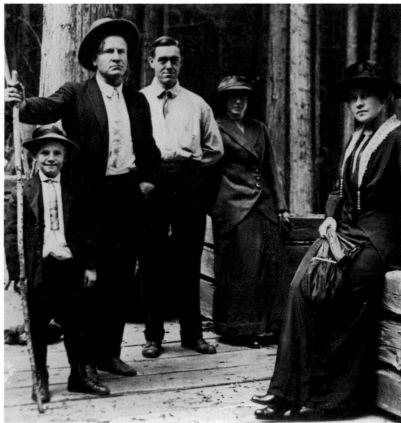

Niedringhaus. After making his fortune in a hardware business, Niedringhaus had invested his money in Texas longhorns and a ranch in Montana. Russell had occasionally worked at this ranch in the mid-1890's. Aware of Russell's reputation, Niedringhaus commissioned several paintings, leaving the price and choice of subject matter entirely up to Russell. This was a turning point in Russell's career; the commission gave him the confidence and financial security to give up cow-herding and thereafter devote his time solely to art. "That fall," he said, "after work was over I left, and I never sang to the hosses and the cattle again."

For the next few years Russell painted steadily. Finding the distractions in Great Falls too much, he retreated to a studio in Cascade, a small town 20 miles upriver. At the time Russell sold his paintings to local clients, and to Niedringhaus, for ridiculously low sums – five to ten dollars each. But he managed to scrape by and amassed a body of work. When in 1893 he returned to Great Falls, he had completed forty watercolors and twenty oils in two years.

In 1895 Russell decided he needed a vacation and visited his old friend, Ben Roberts, in Cascade. It was here that he met his bride-to-be, Nancy Cooper. Although she was only seventeen at the time, and he was thirty-one, they struck up a rapport and a close friendship. Russell had only been in love once before and was unaccustomed to the ways of women. In a letter to his father he wrote, "Cupid has bushwacked me – he shot me when I wasn't lookin'." The two were married on September 1896 in a small ceremony at the Roberts' home.

Charlie's father helped the financially struggling couple by setting them up in a large house in Great Falls. Soon it became apparent that Nancy was able to offer Charlie more than just loving companionship; she became, in actuality, his business partner. She persuaded Charlie to adhere to a regular work schedule and to spend less time carousing with his cronies, who resented her for this. With equal determination, she took control of sales of his work and began charging prices that reflected its real value. She also encouraged him to write stories for publication. Above all, she was a great support to Russell, who often praised his wife with gratitude:

> The lady I trotted in double harness with was the best booster an' pardner a man ever had. She could convince anybody that I was the greatest artist in the world, an' that makes a feller work harder. Y'u jes' can't disappoint a person like that, so I done my best work for her . . . We're pardners, an' if she hadn't prodded me, I wouldn't have done the work I did. An' if it hadn't been for Mame, I wouldn't have had a roof over my head.

In April of 1897 a popular magazine, *Recreation*, published Russell's first story, along with three of his illustrations. Around this time Russell's painting improved dramatically. He was constantly working to improve his skill. At the age of 33 he reached a more mature level in his painting technique. The influence of Charles Wimar was evident in Russell's paintings from this time on. As late as 1920 Wimar was the only important influence that Russell would acknowledge. Whereas before Russell had relied on meticulous draftsmanship, he now used his paint brush more freely, bringing out the details and mood of his subject in richer colors. Moreover, he refined his compositions, carefully placing fewer subjects against the landscape.

Despite Russell's artistic growth, financial success was still slow in coming. Nancy urged him to seek a wider audience in large cities beyond Montana. In the fall of 1903 they went on a trip – first to St. Louis, then to Chicago, where one of his paintings was accepted for exhibition at the World's Fair. From there, they made their way to New York.

In New York, Russell enjoyed meeting a number of artists

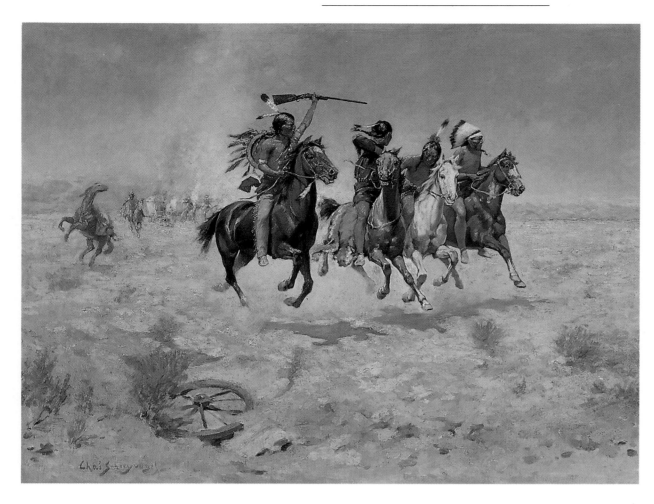

and entertainers. These included another western painter, Charles Schreyvogel, and comedian Will Rogers, who over the years became a close friend of Russell's. At social gatherings Russell received a good many stares when wearing his usual red sash and cowboy boots; But once he would start talking, he captivated everyone with his stories of the West. All in all, Russell was not particularly impressed with the "big camp" as he called New York. As he put it: "It's too big and there are too many tall tepees. I'd rather live in a place where I know somebody and everybody is Somebody."

Meanwhile in New York, Russell was becoming a "Somebody" whom publishers sought for his illustrations. By the following year he illustrated two books – W. T. Hamilton's *My Sixty Years on the Plains*, and B. M. Bower's *Chip of the Flying U.* – as well as a number of magazine articles for *McClure's* and *Leslie's Illustrated Weekly.* He was also chosen to write and illus-

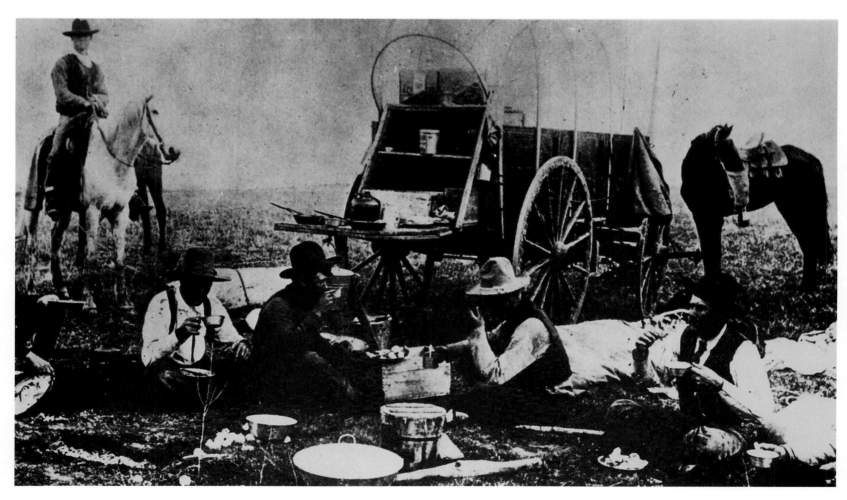

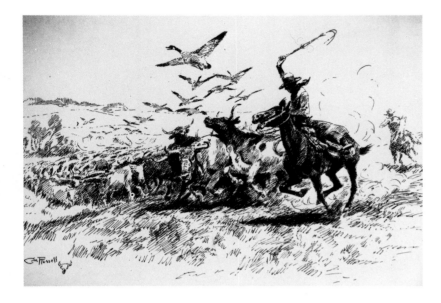

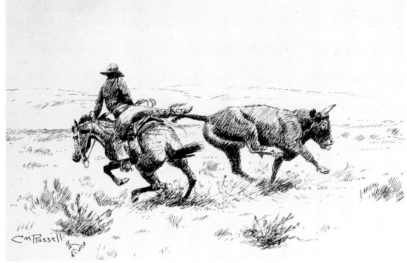

trate a series of short stories, *Line Camp Yarns,* for the prestigious *Outing* magazine. Almost overnight Russell gained a respected niche as an illustrator in the publishing world.

Yet Russell preferred to paint and sculpt for his own satisfaction. He chose scenes and stories that inspired him. One of the best showcases for his work were saloons. The Mint saloon in Great Falls, owned by Sid Willis, became famous for showing large collections of Russell's paintings, sculptures, and drawings. Beginning with his first purchase, *The Hold Up,* Willis amassed over the years one of the largest collections of Russell's work.

Gradually, Russell became regarded as a serious painter as well as an illustrator. In November 1903 he had his first one-man show of his paintings at the Noonan-Kocian Galleries in St. Louis. In 1910 George Niedringhaus organized a special display of oils and watercolors in St. Louis, where one of Russell's finest paintings of intertribal warfare, *When Blackfeet and Sioux Meet,* sold for $800; and one of his most famous cowboy scenes, *In Without Knocking,* sold for $900. These prices amazed Russell. The amounts were certainly a great leap from Russell's prices of ten years earlier but still were minuscule in comparison with the true value of his work.

It took longer to gain acceptance in the East; but in 1909 his exhibition in Brooklyn, New York, broke the ice. By 1911 when the prestigious Folsom Galleries mounted a major Russell show, *The New York Times* devoted almost a full page in its review of the "cowboy artist's" work. Russell had finally arrived.

In July of that year, Russell received official endorsement from his adopted state of Montana – which reached statehood in 1889 – when it commissioned him to paint an immense mural to hang behind the speaker's station in the House of Representatives in the state capitol. This painting of Lewis and Clark's historic meeting with the Ootlashoot Indians is considered to be one of Russell's greatest masterpieces. Although Russell was not daunted by the magnitude of this project, it did present some technical problems; in particular, his studio in Great Falls was not large enough to house the canvas.

So Russell reluctantly decided to expand his treasured log cabin studio. He had built the cabin himself and furnished it with rough-hewn chairs and benches, easels and drawing

boards, and for the floors – buffalo, bear, and wolf skins. On the walls he hung photographs of his friends, numerous gifts of Indian artifacts, and over the door, his prized possession – an old buffalo skull – which became Charlie's trademark as part of his signature on paintings.

Russell's reputation as a western artist crept beyond the boundaries of his own country. In 1912 he was invited to exhibit his work in Canada at the Calgary Stampede; and the following year he prepared a special show in Saskatchewan for the Prince of Wales, who purchased one of his paintings. In 1914 Russell exhibited his work at the Dore Galleries on London's fashionable Bond Street.

While on tour Charlie sent delightful illustrated letters to his friends to fill them in on the new cultural sights he saw. His observations, seen through cowboy eyes, effect a homespun humor so typical of Charlie. For instance, when he visited the

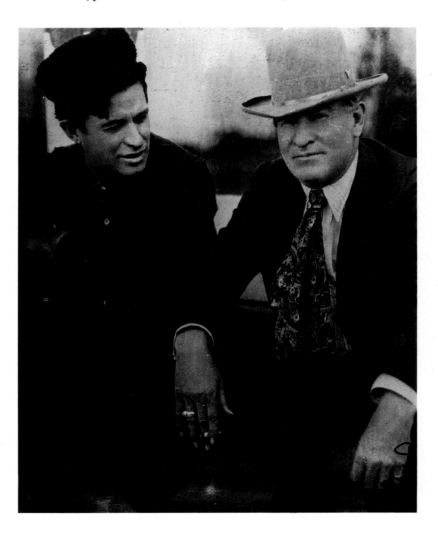

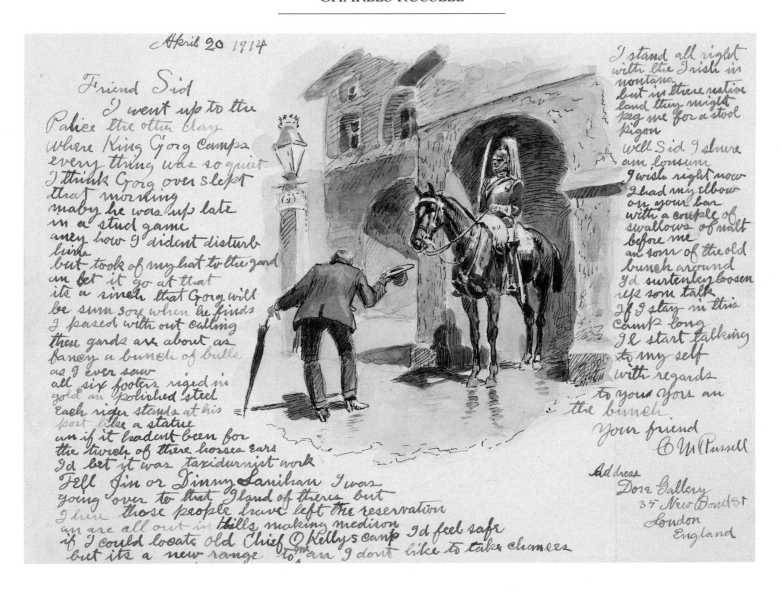

royal palace in London "where King G'org camps," imagine Charlie's reaction to seeing British guards mounted so still upon his favorite animal – the cowboy's vigorous companion, the horse. He wrote Sid Willis:

> . . . these gards are about a fancy a bunch a of bulls as I ever saw; all six footers riged in gold an polished steel; each riger stands at his post like a statue an if it hadent been for the twich of there horses ears id bet it was taxidurnest work.

Russell had won international acclaim. But the one thing that he and Nancy lacked was a child of their own. Russell loved children; he would often play with them for hours, making models and telling them stories of his adventures in the West. When in 1916 he and Nancy adopted a boy, Russell bubbled over with joy. He wrote to a friend: "He was a little two month slickear when we put our iron on him. His name is Jack . . . so he's ours all right and we shure love him."

Russell had reached the pinnacle of his career. His work was constantly in demand and selling for increasingly high prices. In 1921 Russell collected the highest price ever paid for the work of a living American artist of the time – when Nancy sold one of his small paintings for $10,000. In 1925 Russell had exhibitions in every major city, from Los Angeles to New York to Washington, D.C., where in 1925 Russell exhibited at the famed Corcoran Gallery. He received unequivocal praise from cowboys, Indians, critics, artists and even academics. In 1925 the University of Montana bestowed upon Charlie – a man who had never learned how to spell – an honorary degree of Doctor of Law.

As the Old West passed before his eyes – the Indians driven into remote and arid corners of the country, railroads crossed prairies now cut with barbed wire, buffalo extinct and cattle

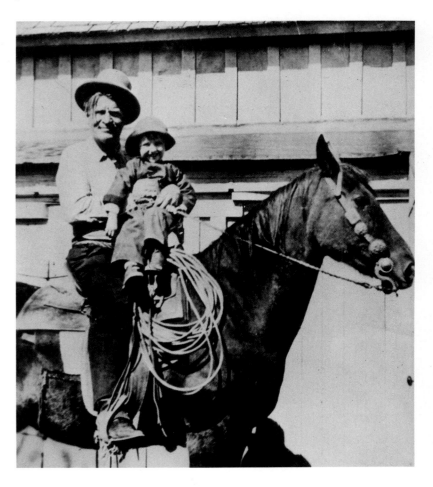

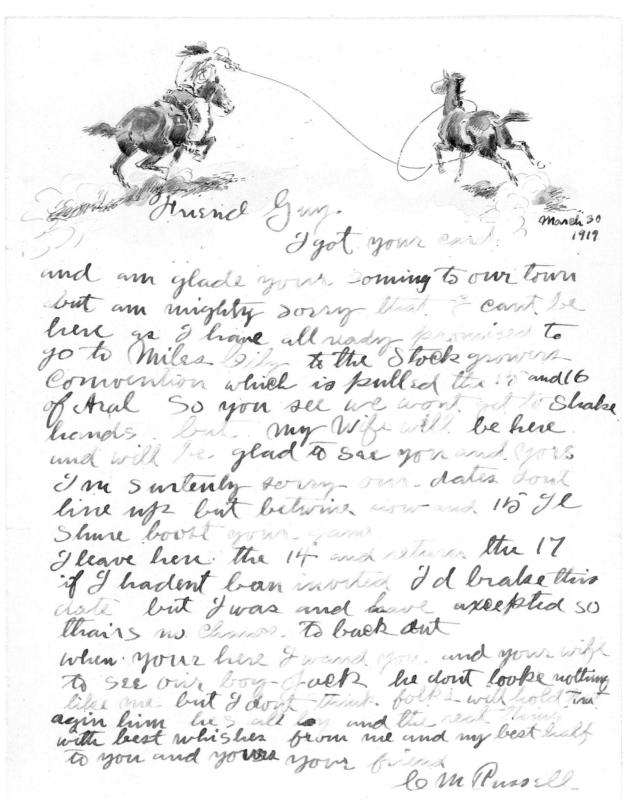

confined to the mountains, and the wild horses he loved so much rounded up and slaughtered – Russell increasingly relied upon memory to create his artistic impressions of the frontier. In his exhibitions he sometimes referred to himself as the "Cowboy Painter of the West that has Passed." Once when a British reporter asked him why he exhibited under that title, Charlie replied wistfully: "Waal, the life that I went out to has passed. Your hoss was everything in those times. No railways – nothing. But now the prairie's been civilized out of all knowledge." His art is significant for more than its accurate rendition of life on the open plains; it swells with Russell's deep love, understanding and nostalgia of the West.

Russell had achieved all and more than he had ever hoped. After he was informed that he had a weak heart and only a few months to live, Russell acknowledged his gratitude for life in his good-natured way: "Any time I cash in now," he said, "I

win." When he died of a heart attack on October 24, 1926, many mourned the passing of not only a great artist, but a modest, warm and generous man.

Amidst all the praise for Russells' art, a fitting tribute to Russell the man was paid by the humorist Irvin S. Cobb:

> Of the spirit of the man, the essence of him, the soul of him, I could write a book and not say the half of what I'd like to say. A keen but gentle philosophy, a gorgeous darting wit which tickled but never stung; a lover of natural things and of genuine things; a lover of friendships and of children, and of horses and dogs – yes and underdogs; a genius whose culture came not out of books but out of the heart of a born gentleman; a man who could be proud of his talent without being conceited over it; a creature as free from guile, vanity, selfishness and affectation as any I ever knew – that was your Charley Russell.

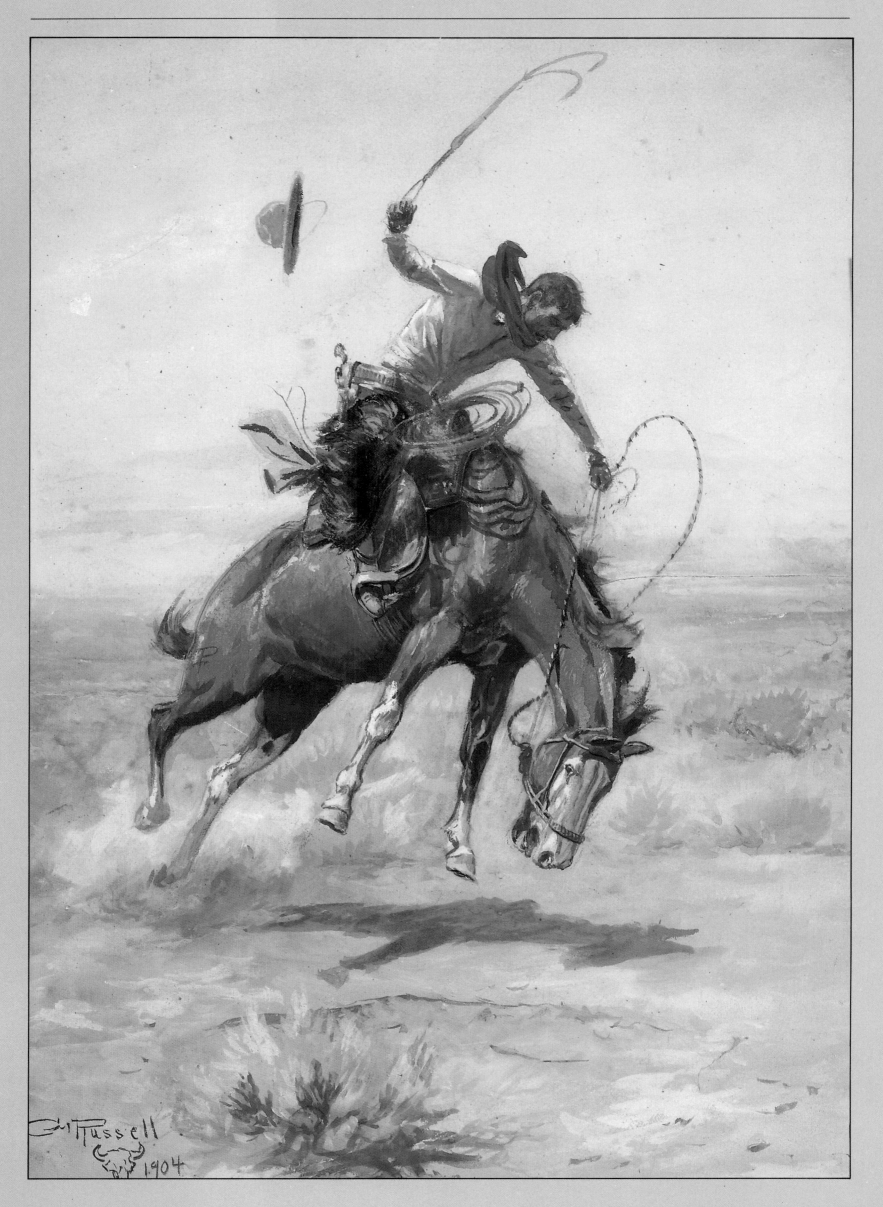

COWBOYS

Charles Russell worked as a horse wrangler and night herder on some of the largest and longest cattle drives in Montana. In the 1880s cattle roundup teams were in demand. In those days ranchers allowed their cattle to roam the open expanses of the fenceless range to forage during the winter. By the spring, the cattle owners had to separate the various herds which were widely scattered and mixed up. Thus, cowboys were hired to roundup the herds and identify the new crop of calves with the brands of each respective owner. Through the summer, as the cattle gained weight grazing, cowboys guarded the herds from the danger of stampedes or rustlers. At the same time, the cowboys drove the herds hundreds of miles to designated train stations in what was called the fall "beef roundup"; in turn, the steer were shipped by rail to stockyards in the East where demand for beef was high.

His own cow-herding experiences, and those of his old cowhand friends, served to inspire Charlie's numerous cowboy scenes. For example, his painting, *Roundup No. 2*, captures one of the most exciting aspects of cowboy life – the roping and throwing of calves for branding; such activities required expert horsemanship and keen eye-hand coordination. Other paintings – *The Strenuous Life, Smokin' 'em Out*, and *Loops and Swift Horses Are Surer than Lead* – depict the rigors involved in managing restless and testy steer, in addition to protecting them from wild animals. Cattle and horse thieves were another type of predator. *When Horse Flesh Comes High* and *Paying the Fiddler* illustrate how cowboy vigilantes dealt with rustlers.

Scenes such as *Cowboy Camp During the Roundup* and *Utica* portray the freewheeling side of the cowboy, who played just as hard as he worked. Cowboys knew how to have a rousing good time, blasting into towns with rounds of gunfire, drinking and storytelling in saloons, busting broncos and picking fights. Just for sport, cowboy toughs would harass a man by making him dance to the beat of their shooting revolvers. *The Tenderfoot* displays this bit of cowboy entertainment. Both this painting and *Utica* reveal Russell's customary attention to detail, to the point that actual cowboy friends and acquaintances of Russell's are recognizable in the picture. In *Utica*, Charlie himself appears as the fellow leaning against the hitching rail just in front of the general store; this store was owned by Walter Lehman, who appears as the bewhiskered fellow standing in the doorway. Lehman was the one who had commissioned this painting as a calendar for his Utica store.

Russell's reputation as the "cowboy artist" is an appropriate one for a man who spent eleven years herding cattle and a lifetime painting, sketching and modeling scenes of western life. The cowboy epitomized the American ideal of rugged individualism and the adventurous spirit of the West. Within his artwork, these cowboys still live the dynamic life that Charlie once enjoyed.

The Bucker
1904, pencil, watercolor and gouache on paper, 16¼×12¼ in.
Sid Richardson Collection of Westion Art, Fort Worth, TX

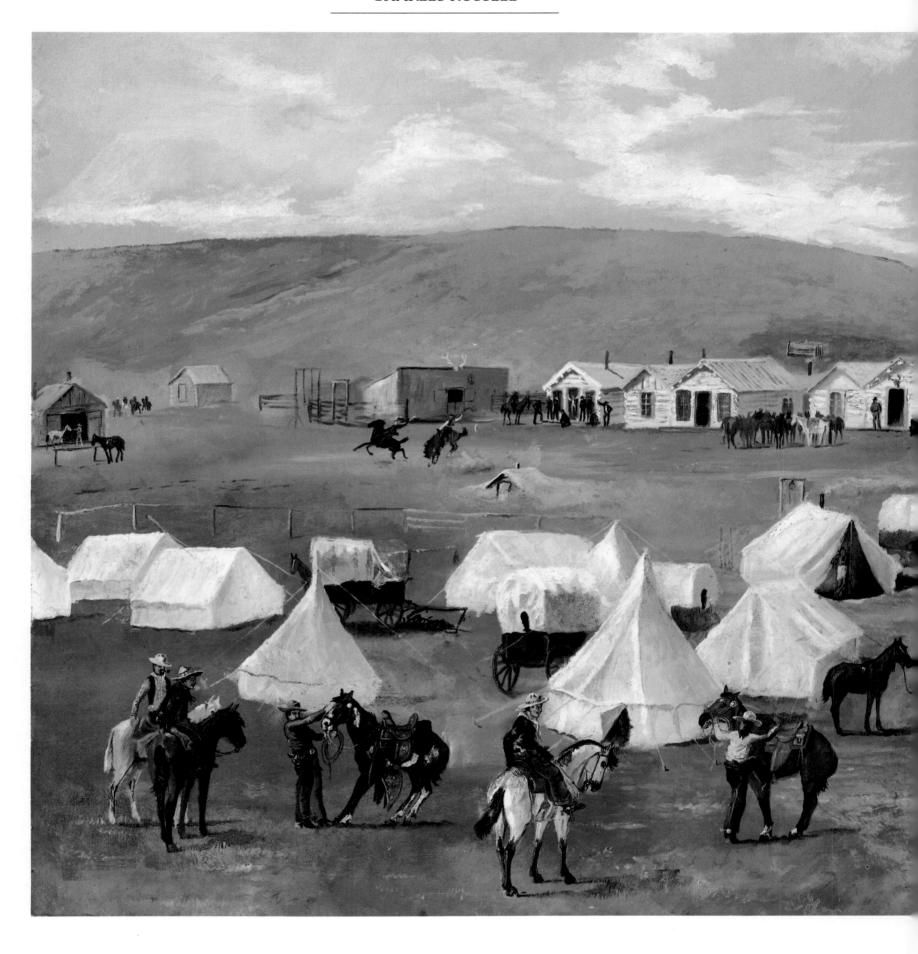

Cowboy Camp During the Roundup
c.1887, oil on canvas, 23½×47¼ in.
Amon Carter Museum, Fort Worth, TX

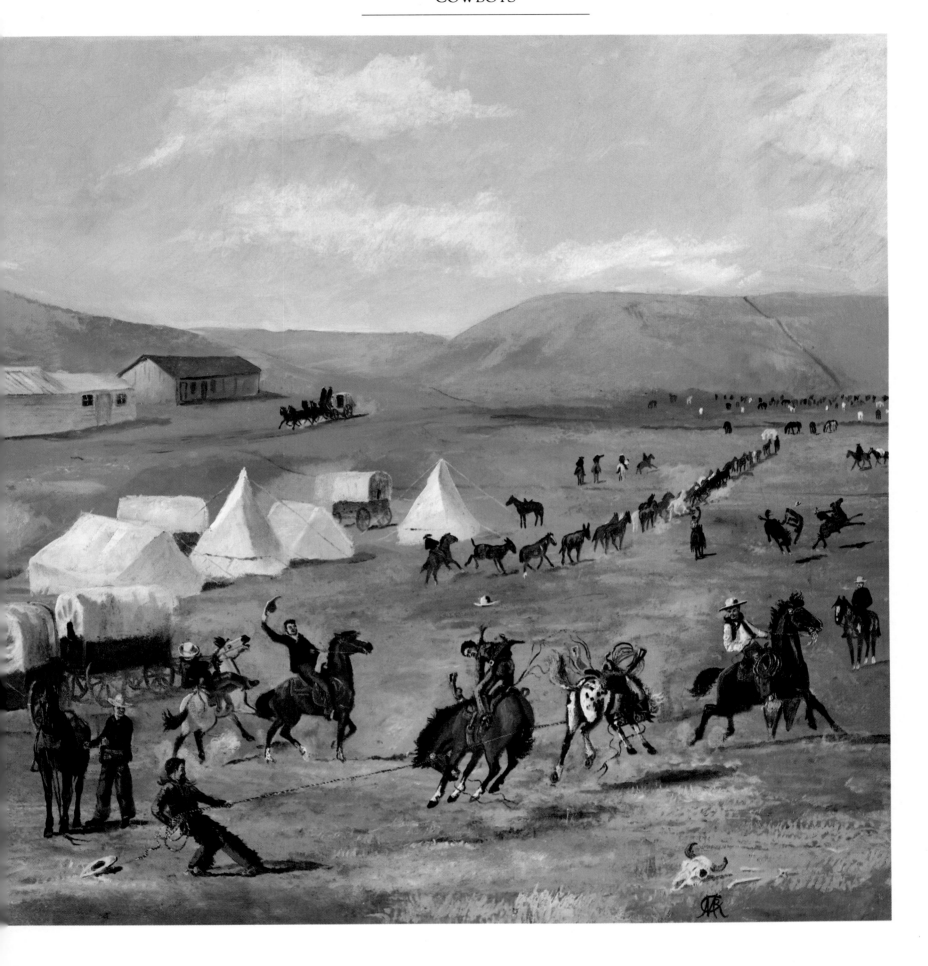

The Herd Quitter
1897, oil on canvas, 20×31 in.
Gift of Colonel Wallis Huidekoper, Montana Historical Society, Helena, MT

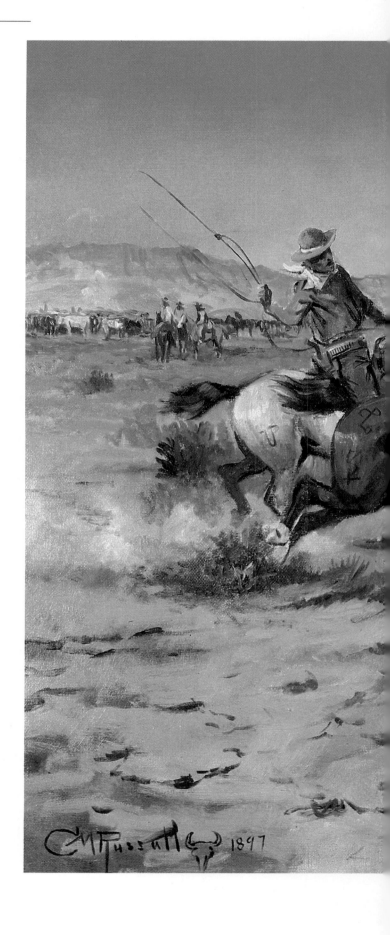

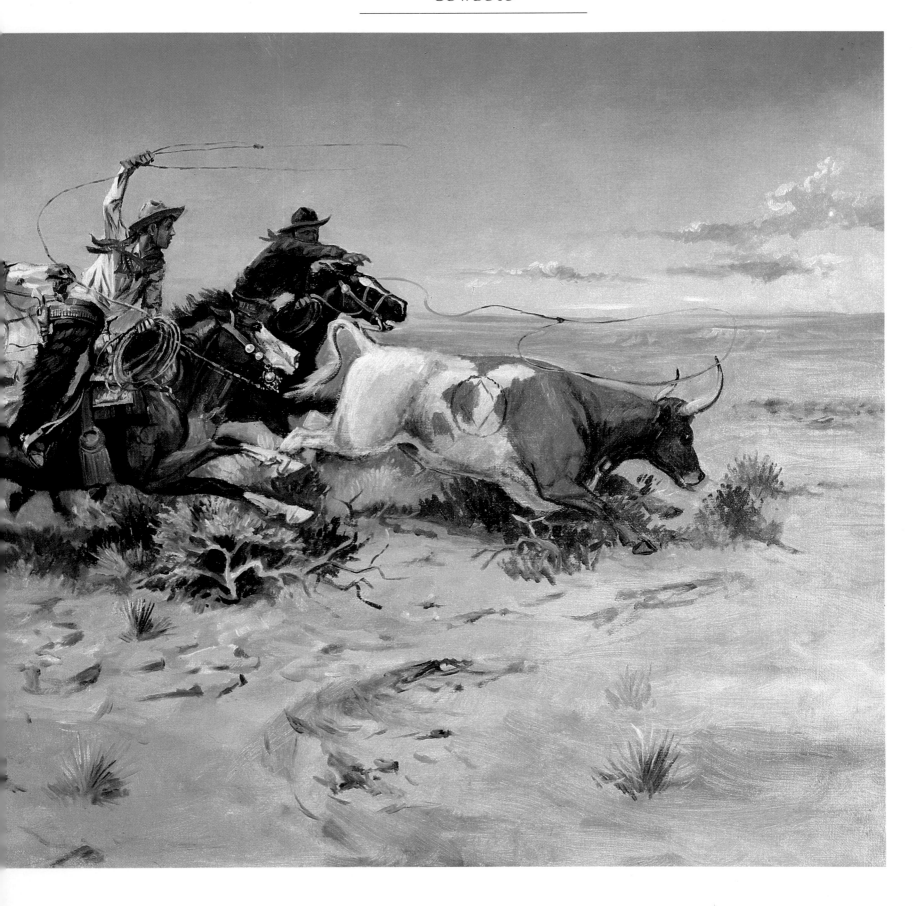

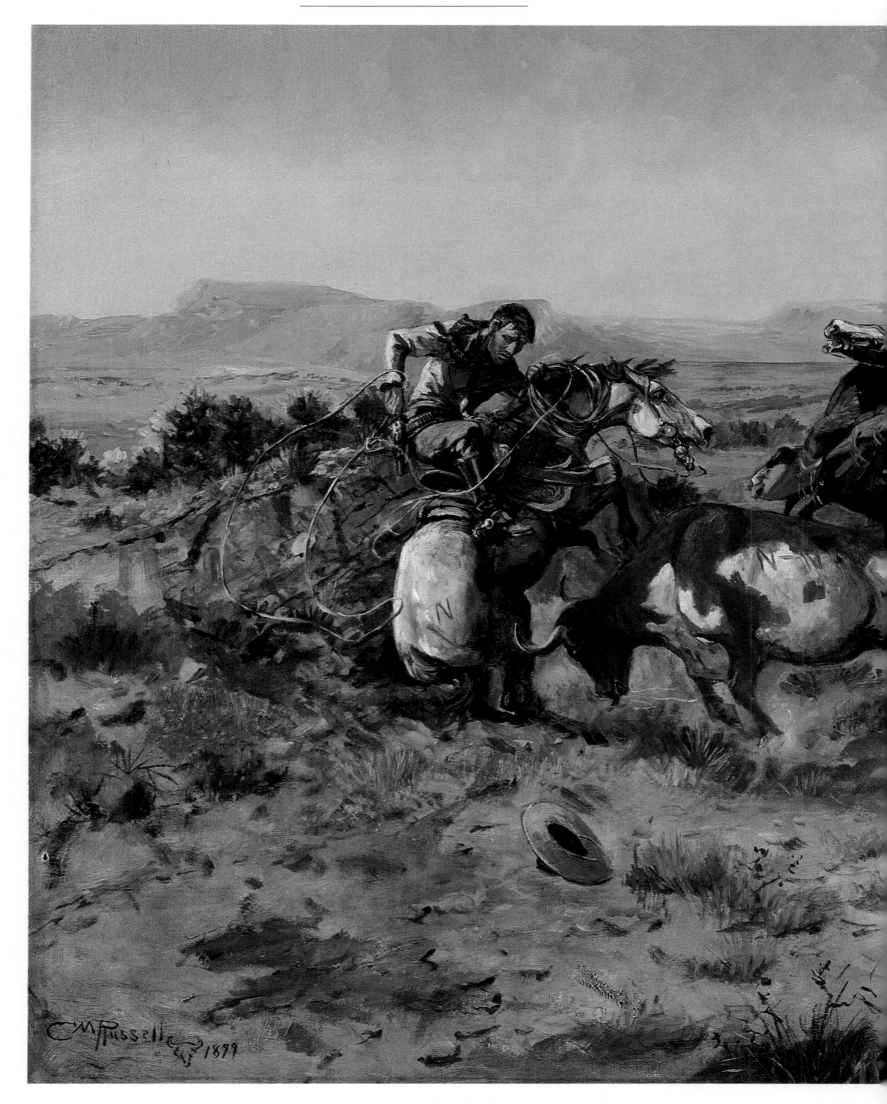

When Cowboys Get in Trouble
1899, oil on canvas, 24×36 in.
Sid Richardson Collection of Western Art, Fort Worth, TX

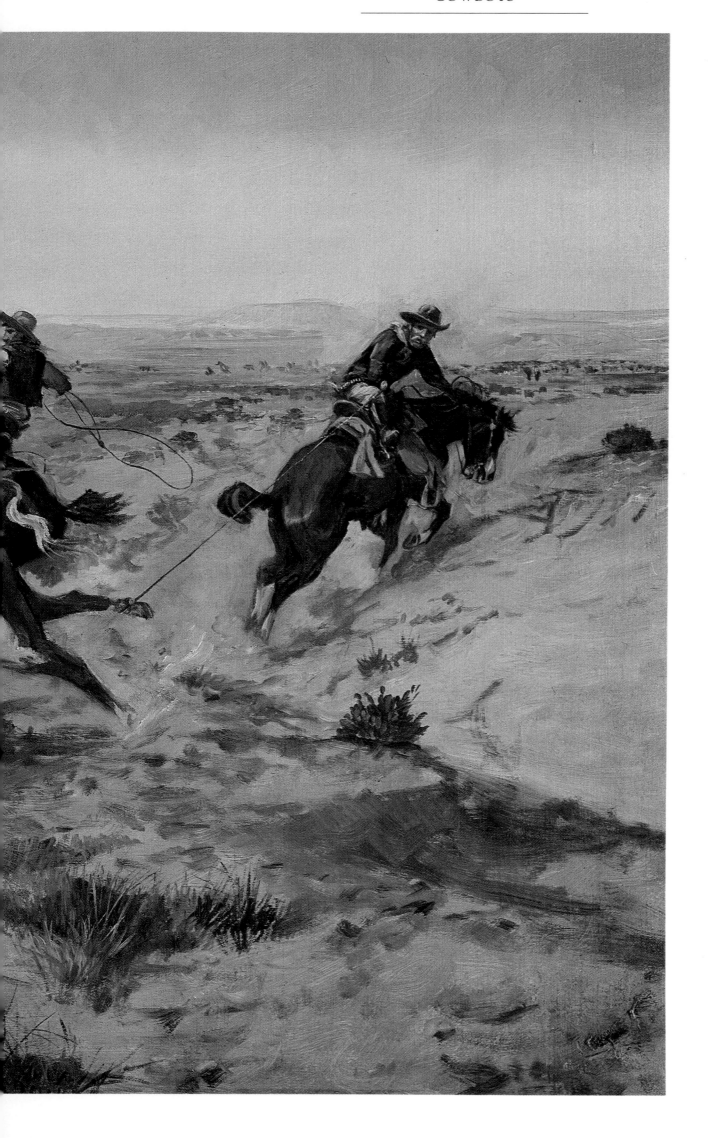

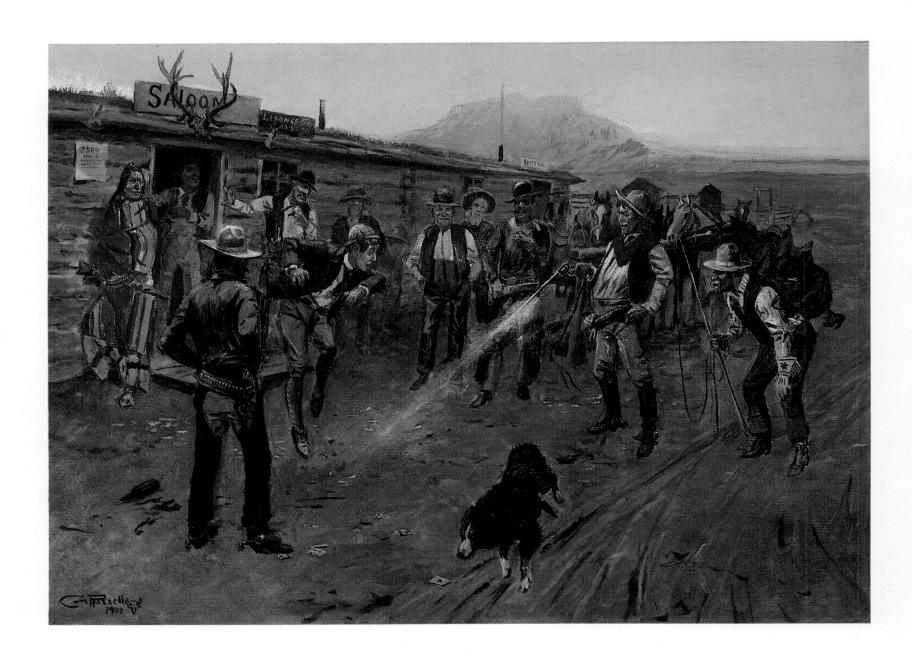

The Tenderfoot
1900, oil on canvas, 14¼×20⅛ in.
Sid Richardson Collection, Fort Worth, TX

Russell on Redbird
1906, watercolor on paper, 12×8¾ in.
C. M. Russell Museum, Great Falls, MT

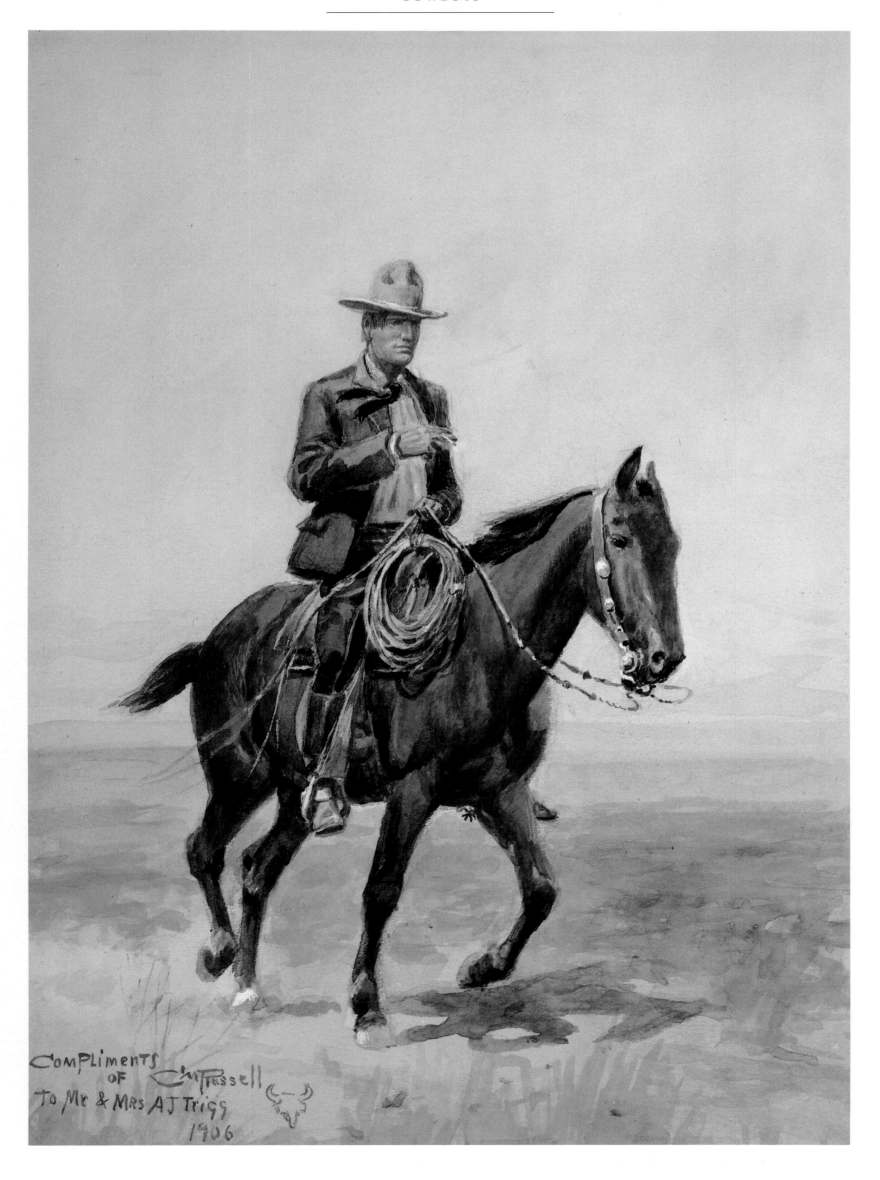

Compliments
of C M Russell
To Mr & Mrs A J Trigg
1906

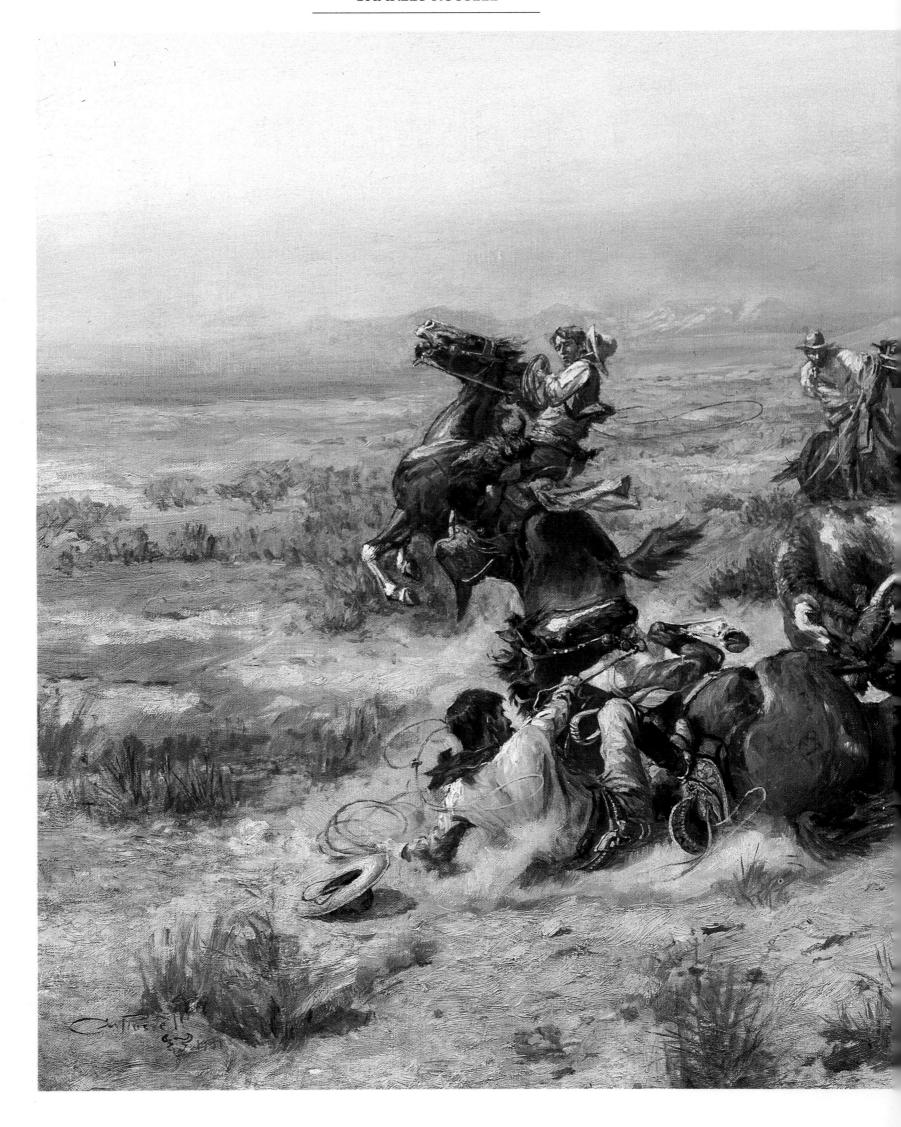

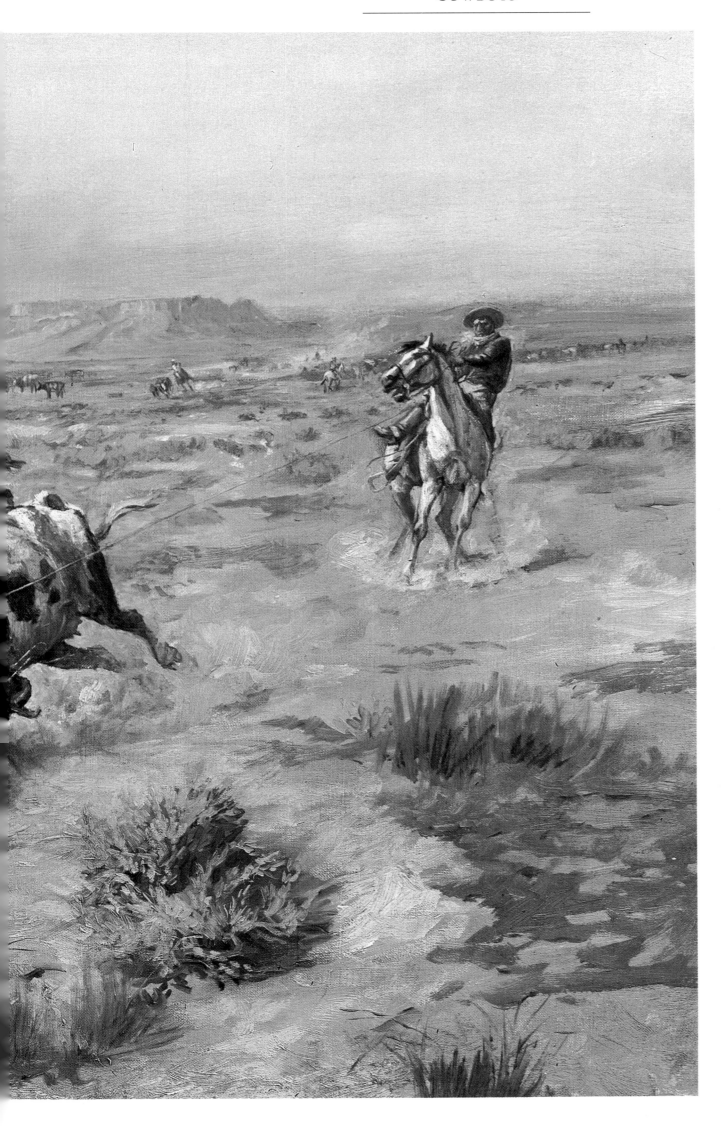

The Strenuous Life
1901, oil on canvas, 36×23 in.
The Thomas Gilcrease Institute of American History and Art, Tulsa, OK

Utica (A Quiet Day in Utica)
1907, oil on canvas, 24⅛×36⅛ in.
Sid Richardson Collection of Western Art,
Fort Worth, TX

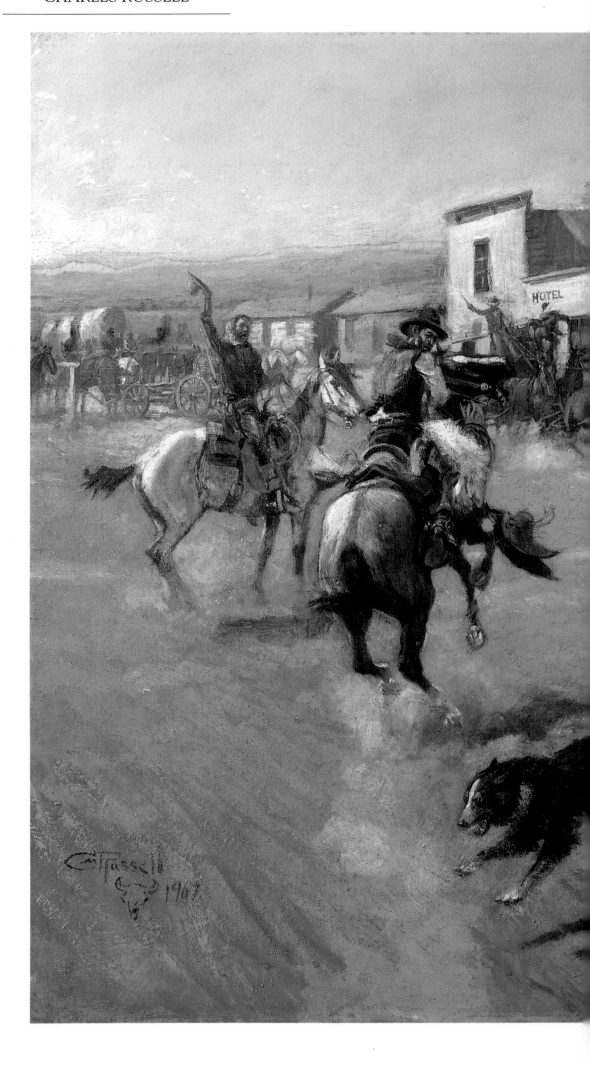

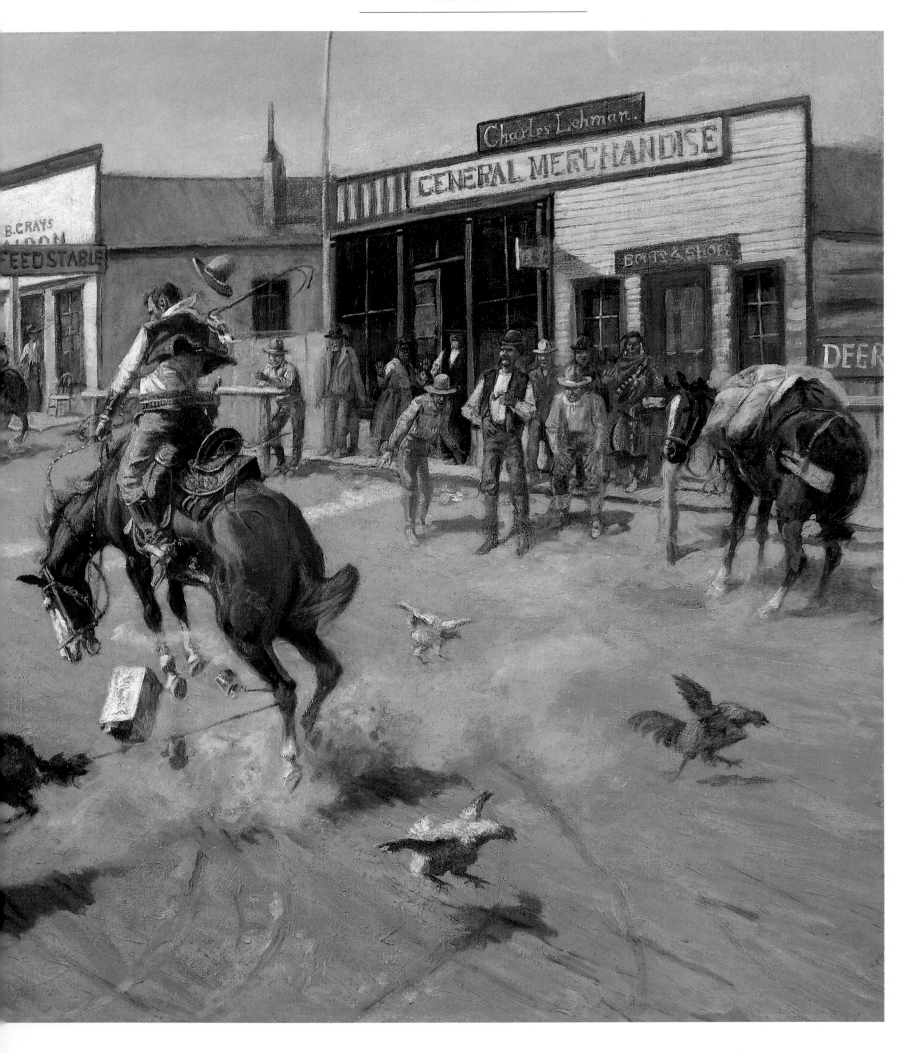

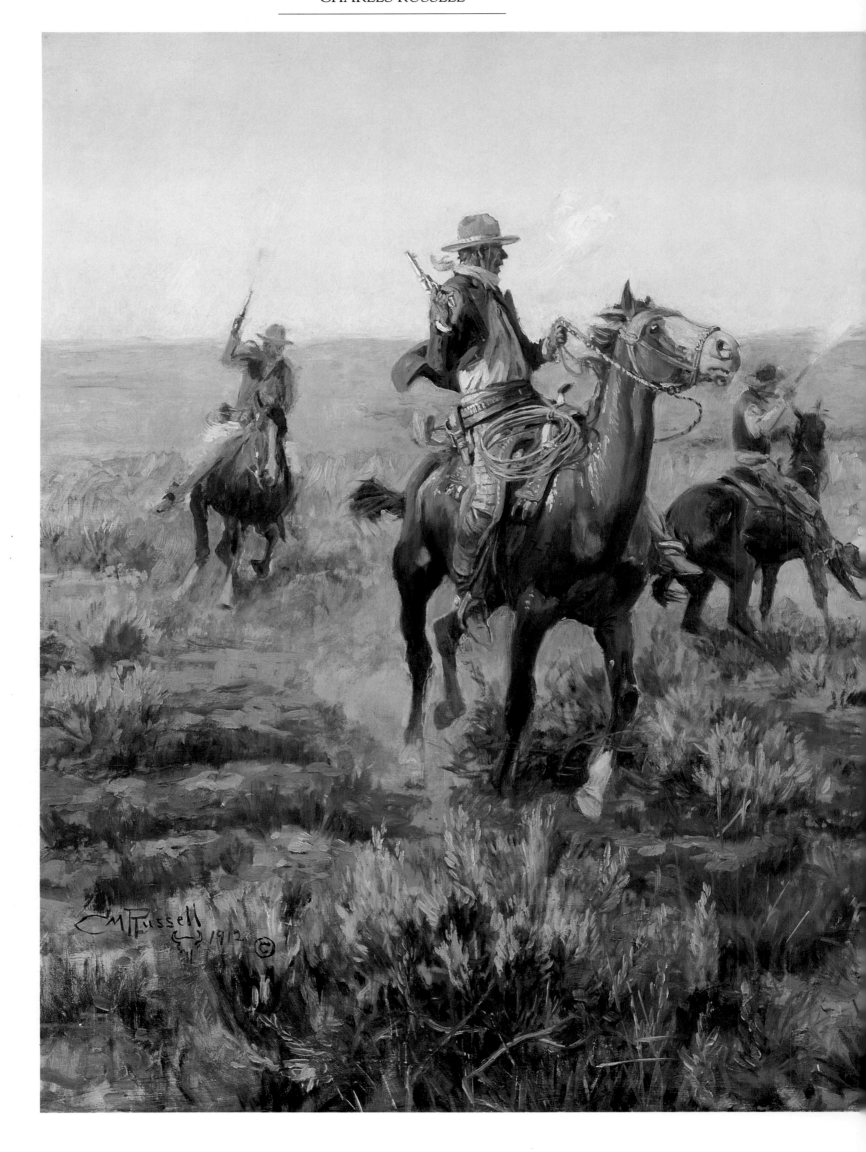

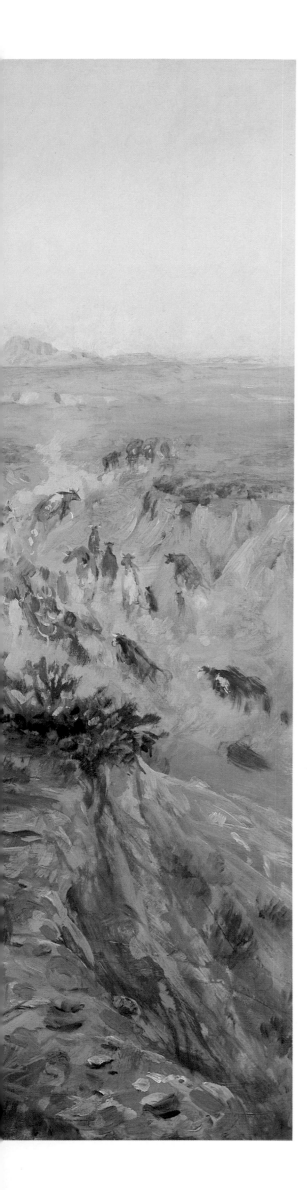

Smokin' 'em Out
1912, oil on linen, 29¼×32½ in.
M. C. Naftzager Collection, Wichita Art Museum, Wichita, KS
© B&B 1942

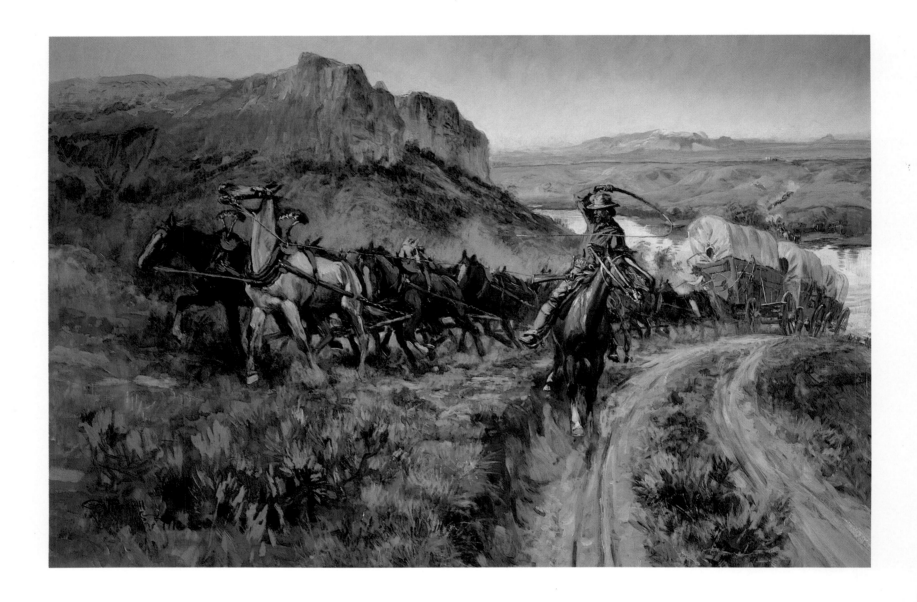

The Jerkline
1912, oil on canvas, 23½×35½ in.
C. M. Russell Museum, Great Falls, MT
© B&B 1947

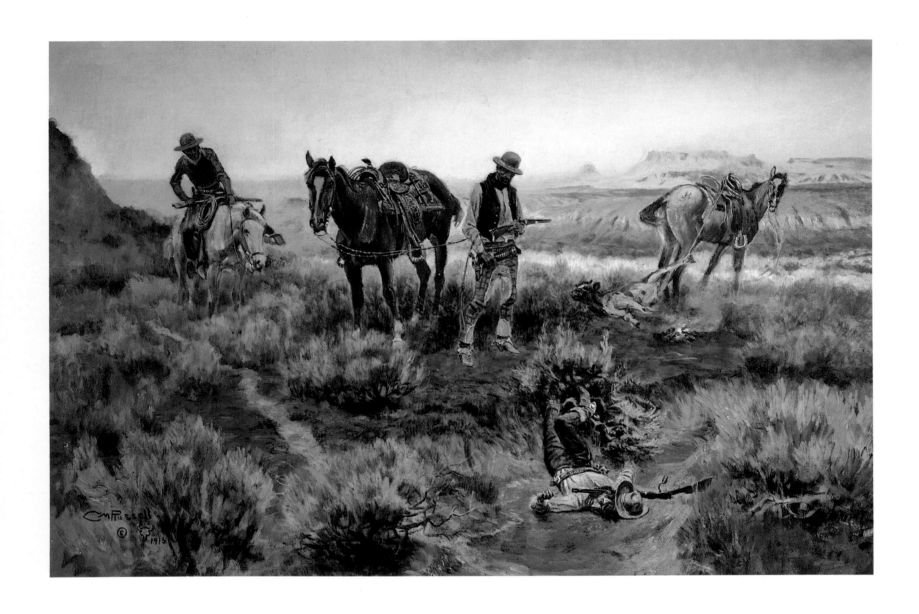

Paying the Fiddler
1919, oil on canvas, 24×36 in.
C. M. Russell Museum, Great Falls, MT

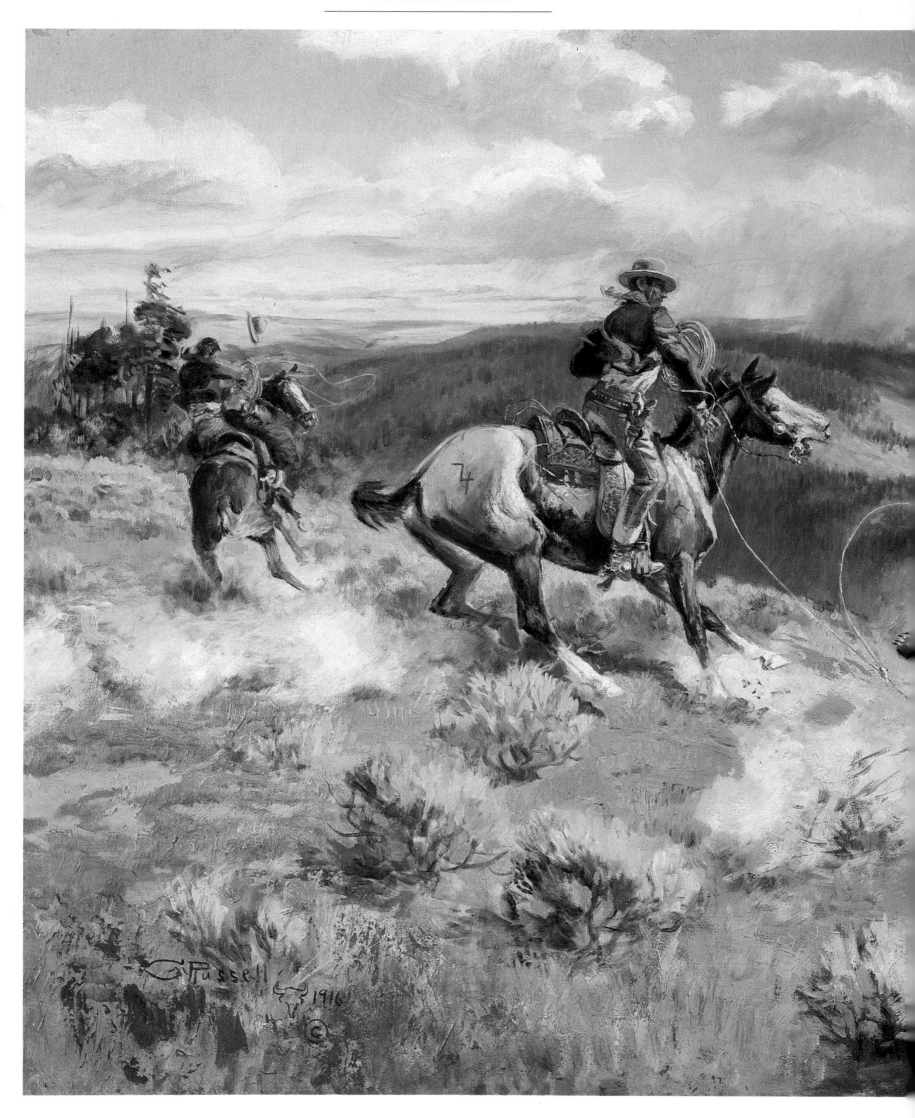

Loops and Swift Horses Are Surer than Lead
1916, oil on canvas, 30¼×48⅛ in.
Amon Carter Museum, Fort Worth, TX

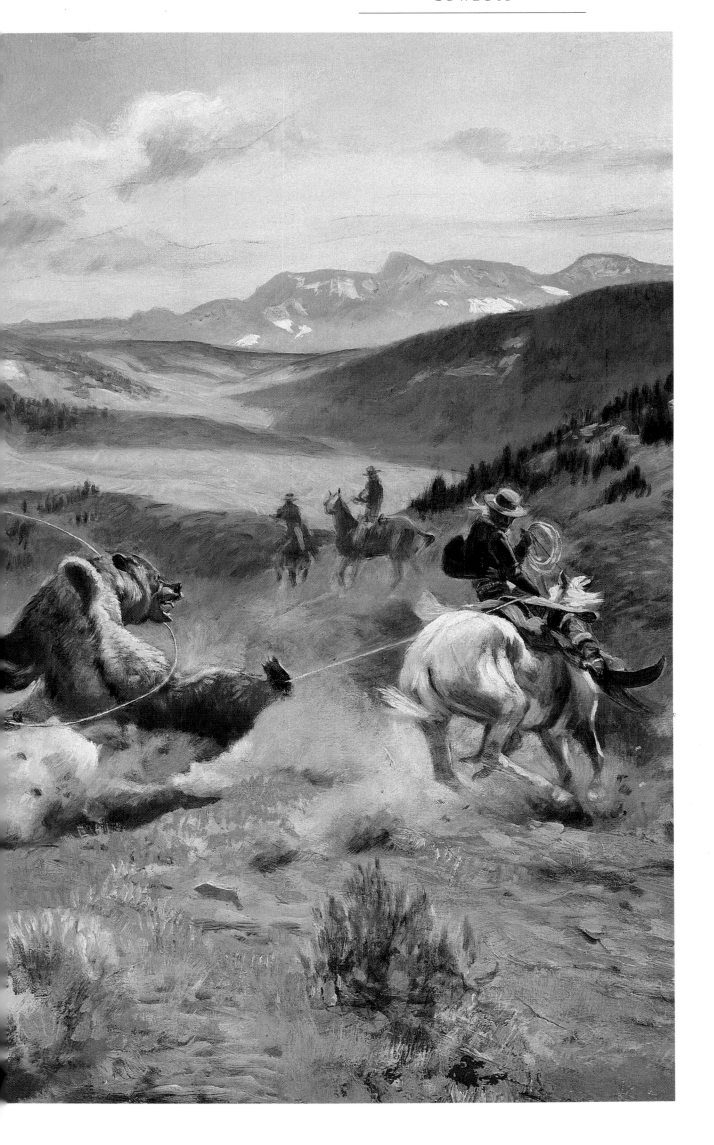

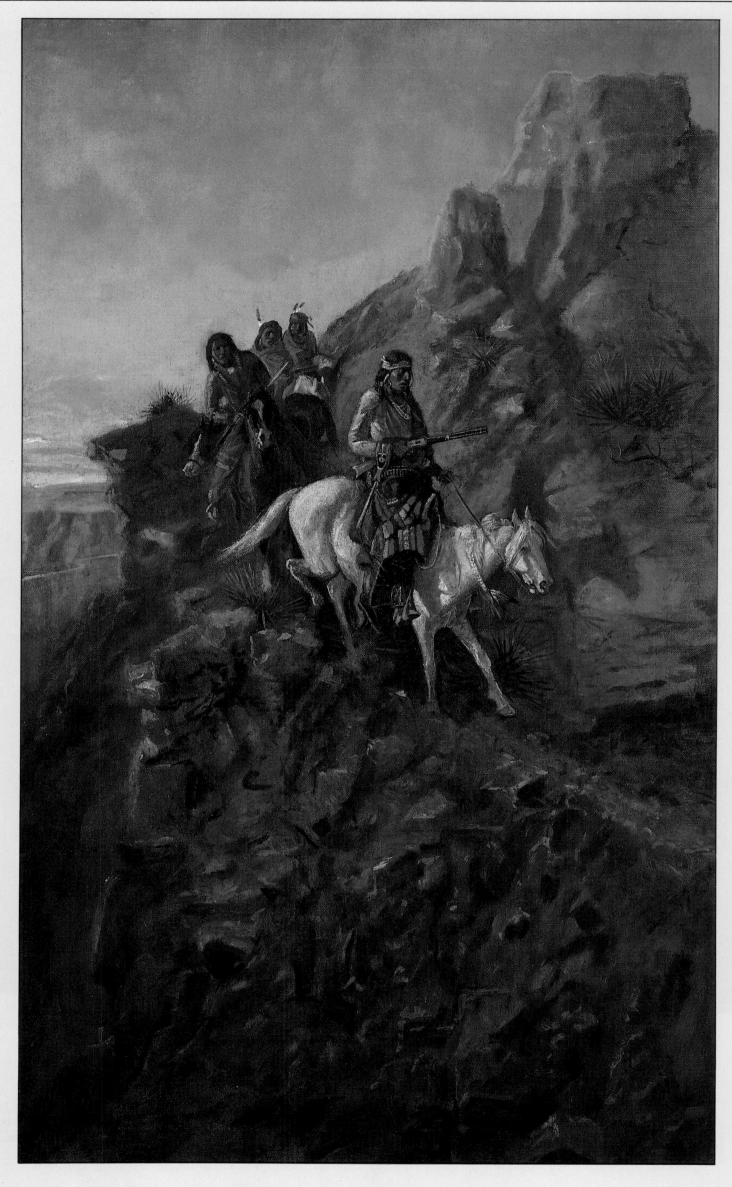

INDIAN LIFE

Charles Russell not only knew and understood the Indians better than most white men of his day, he loved them as his own "red brothers." The dignified ways of the native Americans had always attracted him and he went out of his way to make contact with them. His first opportunity came in the fall of 1888 when he lived in Canada for six months with the Bloods, one of the three tribes of the great Blackfoot nation. Accepted as one of their tribe, he received the honored name of Ah-Wah-Cous, or Antelope. He immersed himself in their culture, learning their language, customs, habits, and religious rituals. He hunted with the Bloods during the day and sat with them by the campfire at night; with reverance he listened to their legends, passed down from each generation, and their stories of the days when they were free to roam the West. Later, Charlie also frequented the reservations of other tribes such as the Arapaho, Kootenai and Crow, and he became proficient in the intertribal language of "sign talk."

Drawing upon this storehouse of experiences with his red brothers, Russell portrayed the Indians with both realism and compassion. For example, Russell painted dynamic scenes of authentic Indian warfare. In his painting *When Blackfeet and Sioux Meet*, he dramatized the intertribal concept of "counting coup" by depicting a Blackfoot brave striking a Sioux warrior, while the other Blackfoot is poised with his tomahawk to take the scalp. It was understood in counting coup that the first warrior to strike his enemy was entitled to the opponent's scalp. Whether the enemy was alive or already dead, the warrior would retrieve the scalp, a custom tied to his religious belief that the spirit of the individual resided in the hair.

Russell also depicted the earthy simplicity and tranquility of Indian life in such paintings as *Bringing Up the Trail* and *The Medicine Man*. These two works depict how the plains Indians migrated from season to season in search of new hunting grounds. Bison, in particular, was critical to the subsistence of these Indians who used parts of the animal in everything from teepees to clothing to food. Russell's *The Silk Robe* is an account of how a buffalo hide was fleshed to be made into a garment. When entire Indian villages picked up and moved with the buffalo supply, scouts would lead the entourage, followed by the men of the tribe, and women and children trailed behind. His many paintings and sketches of Indians hunting bison – sixty in all – underscore the importance of this species to the survival of the Indians.

The authentic detail with which Russell painted the distinguishing traits of the various tribes – from the symbols of the beadwork on their clothes to their methods of warfare – impressed even the Indians. They called him the "picture writer" and thought that his talent was magic, or "good medicine." Russell's affinity with the Indian was also reflected in his physical appearance; when dressed in Indian garb, his acquiline features and stoic manner likened him to a red man more than a white man. Moreover, Russell felt much sympathy for the plight of the Indians in losing their lands and culture, and he respected them as much, and often more, than he did his own race. His paintings, such as *The Fireboat* and *Signal Smoke*, evoke the enmity and tension that the Indian felt toward the encroaching white man. As Russell commented:

> I've known some bad Injuns, but for every bad one I kin match 'im with ten worse white men . . . No Injun ever done me dirt. Many a one's done me favors. When he's a good friend, he's the best friend in the world. White men's whiskey caused all the Injun troubles in the West.

There May Be Danger Ahead
1893, oil on canvas, 36¼×22 in.
Sid Richardson Collection of Western Art, Fort Worth, TX

Crow Indians Hunting Elk
c.1887, oil on canvas, 18⅛×24 in.
Amon Carter Museum, Fort Worth, TX

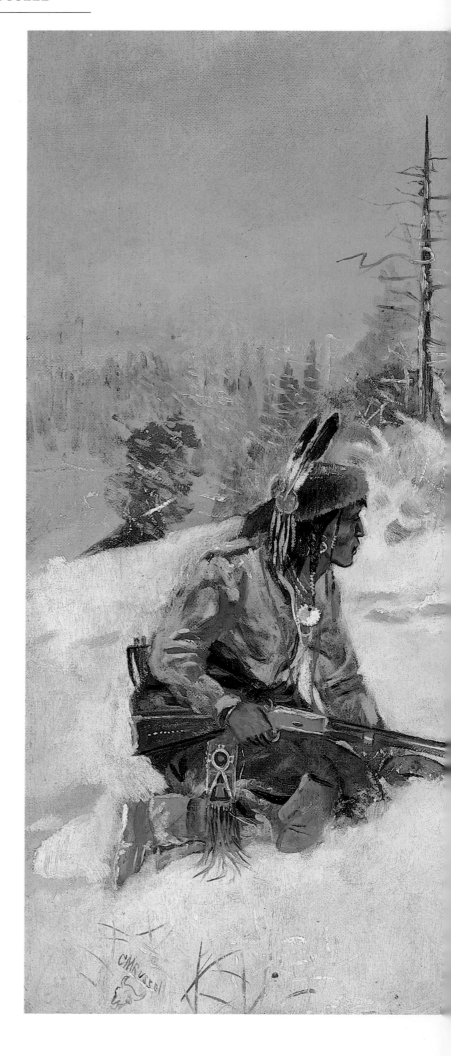

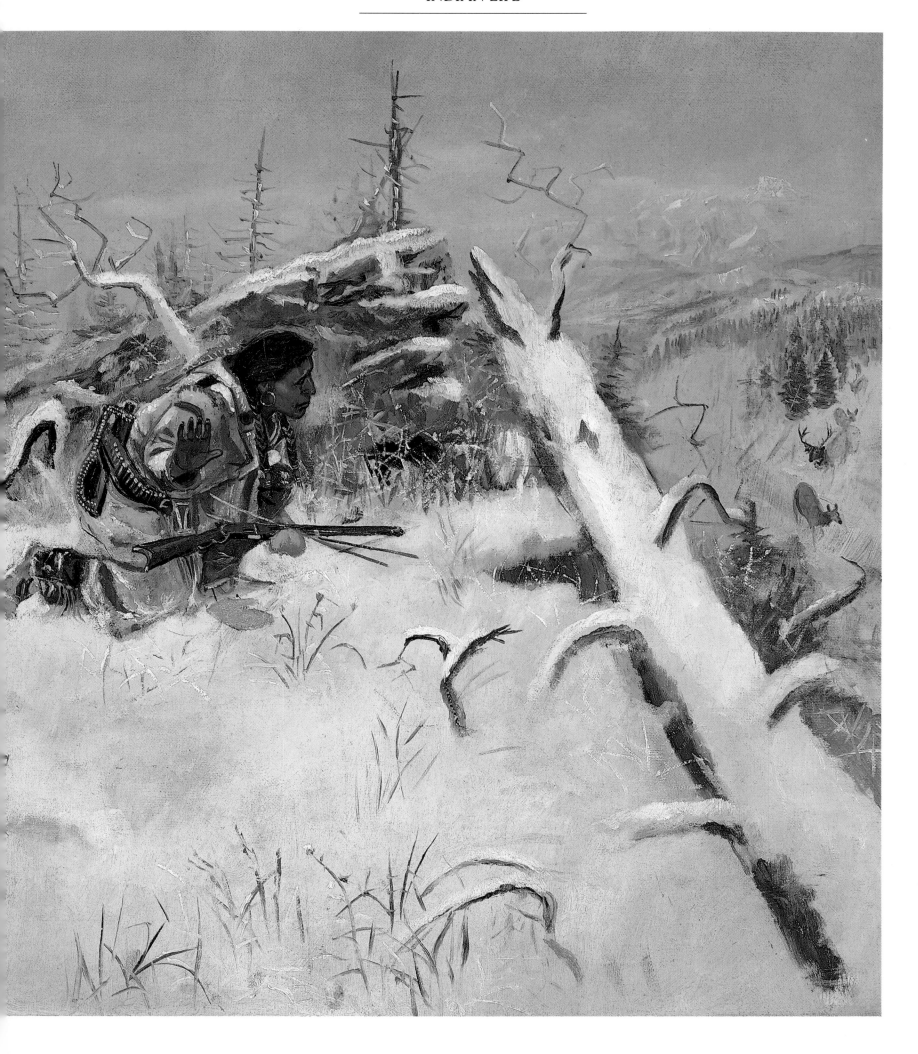

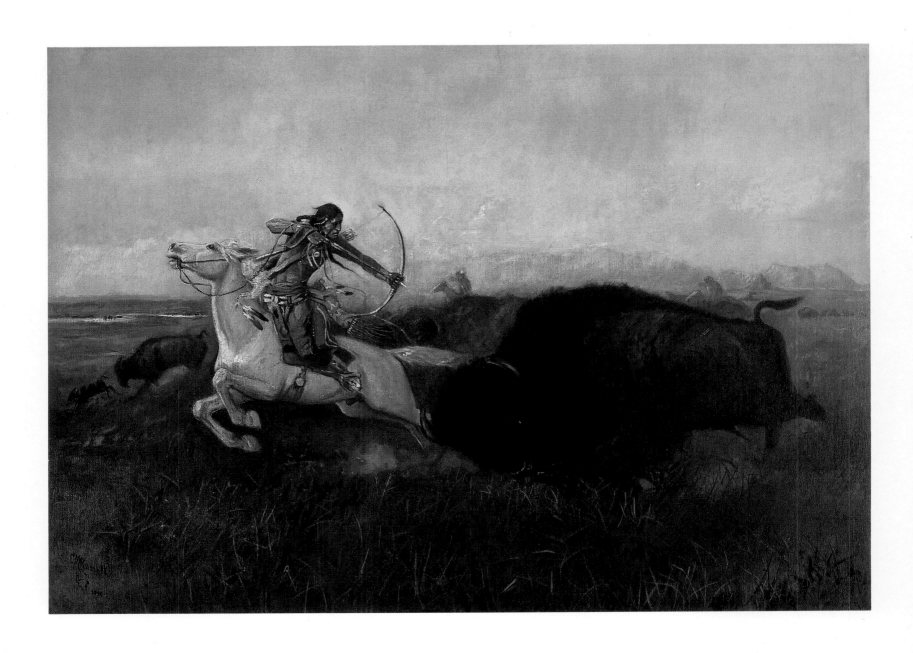

Indians Hunting Buffalo
1894, oil on canvas, 24⅛×36⅛ in.
Sid Richardson Collection of Western Art, Fort Worth, TX

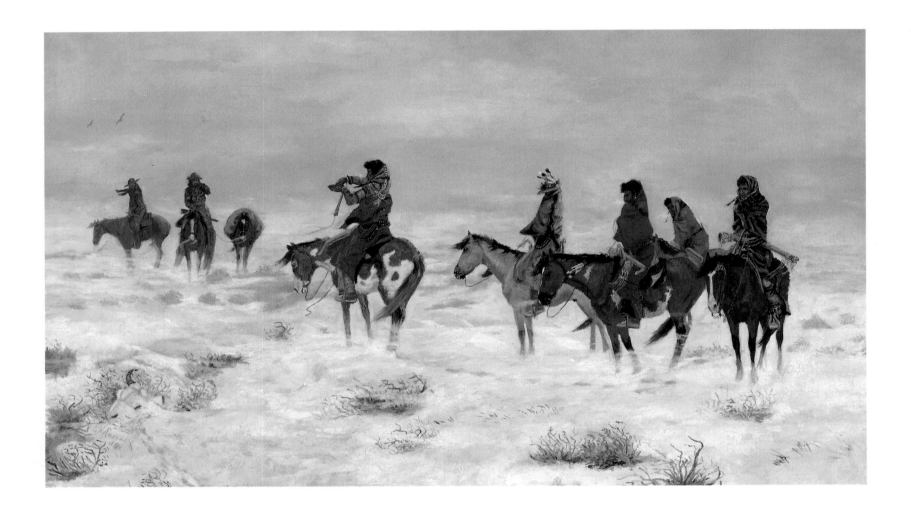

Lost in a Snowstorm – We Are Friends
1888, oil on canvas, 24×43⅛ in.
Amon Carter Museum, Fort Worth, TX

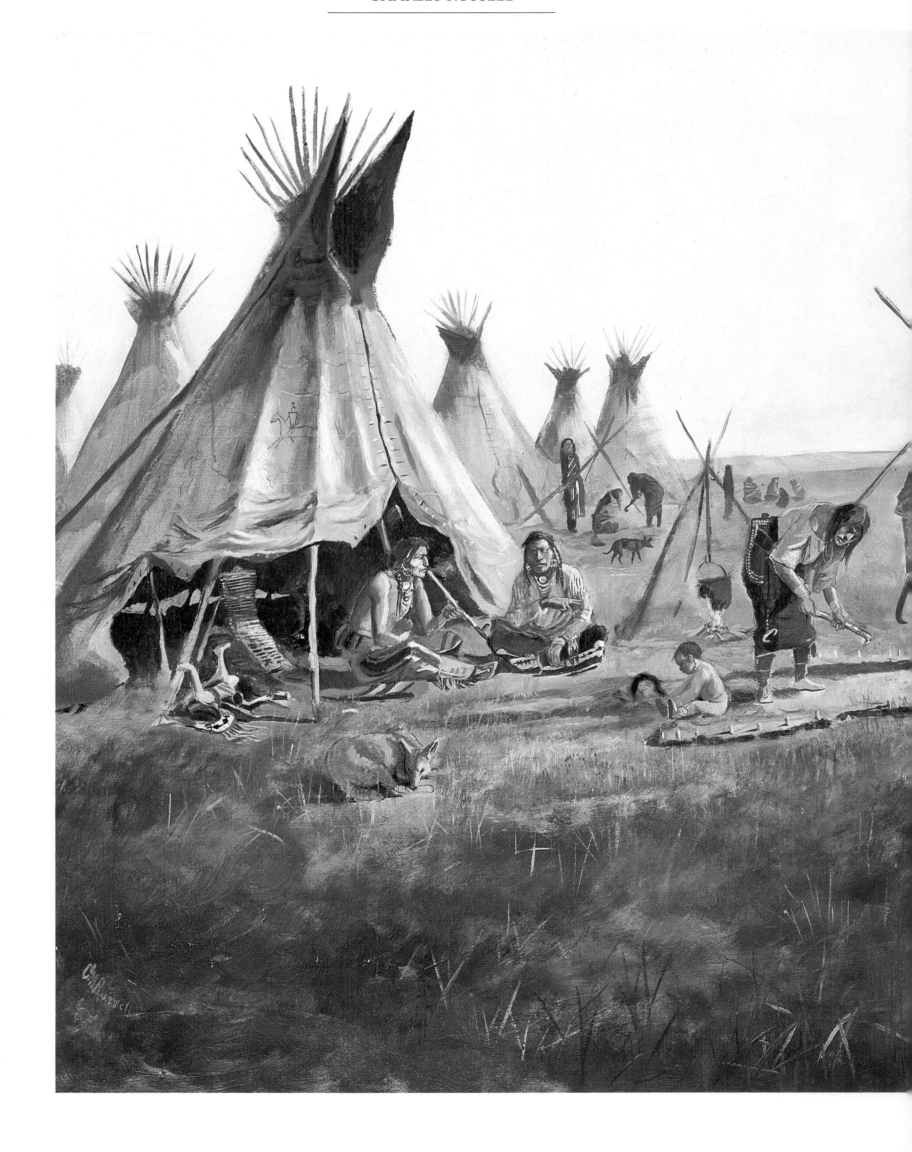

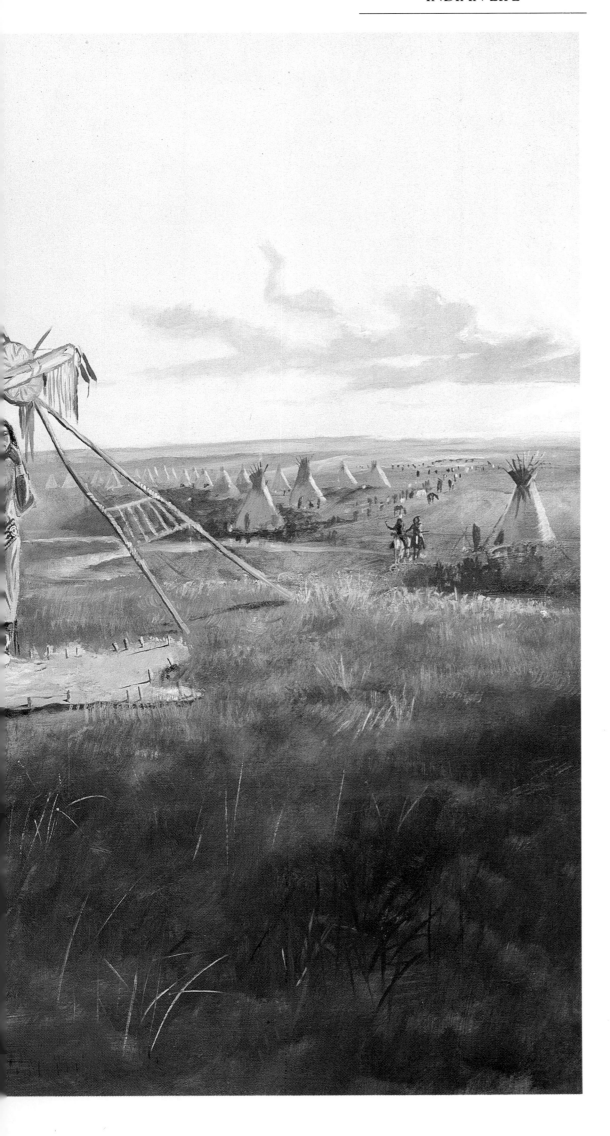

The Silk Robe
c.1890, oil on canvas, 27⅝×39⅛ in.
Amon Carter Museum, Fort Worth, TX

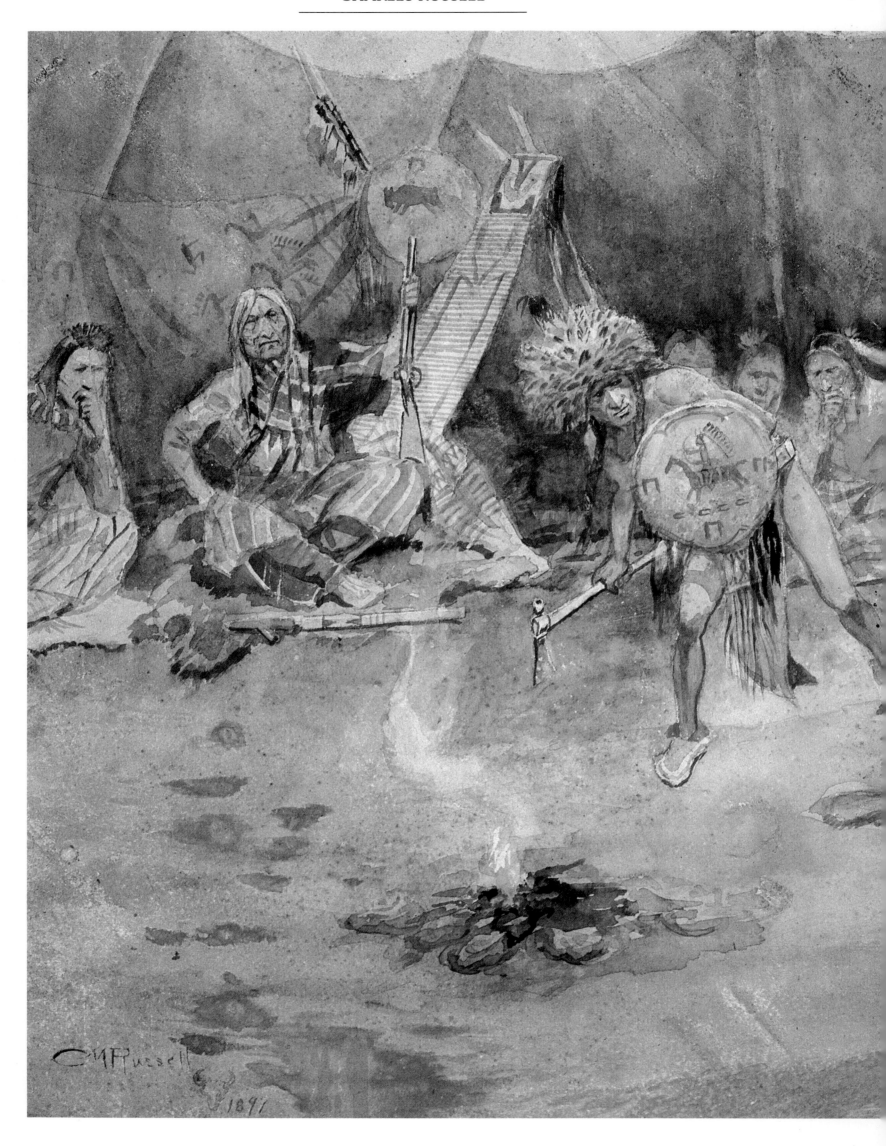

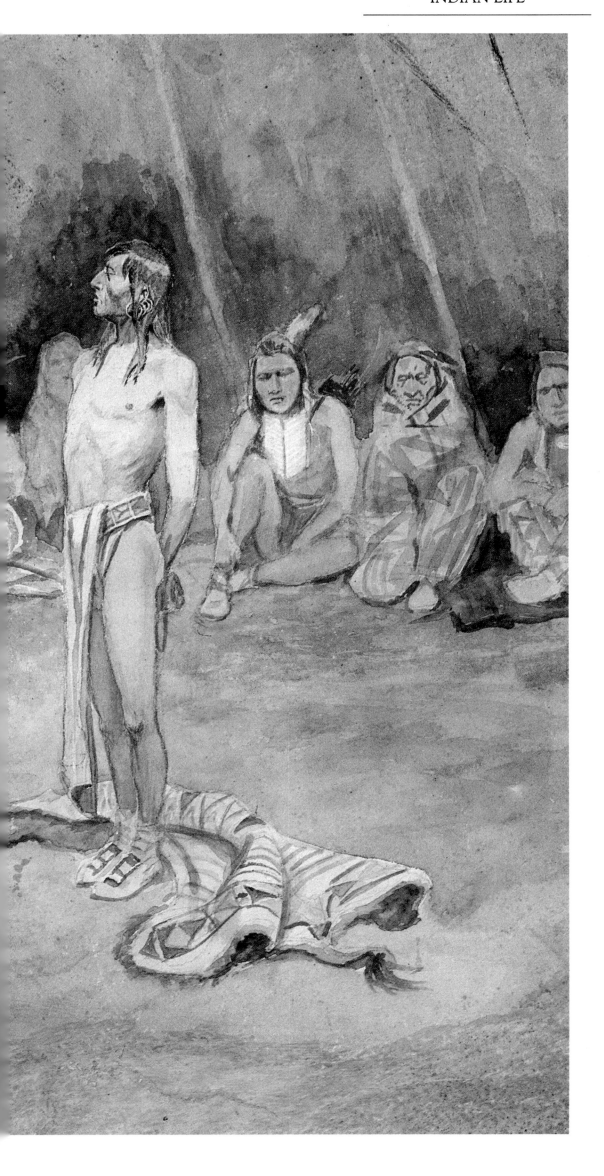

Sioux Torturing a Blackfoot Brave
1891, watercolor, 15×20¼ in
Buffalo Bill Historical Center, Cody, WY

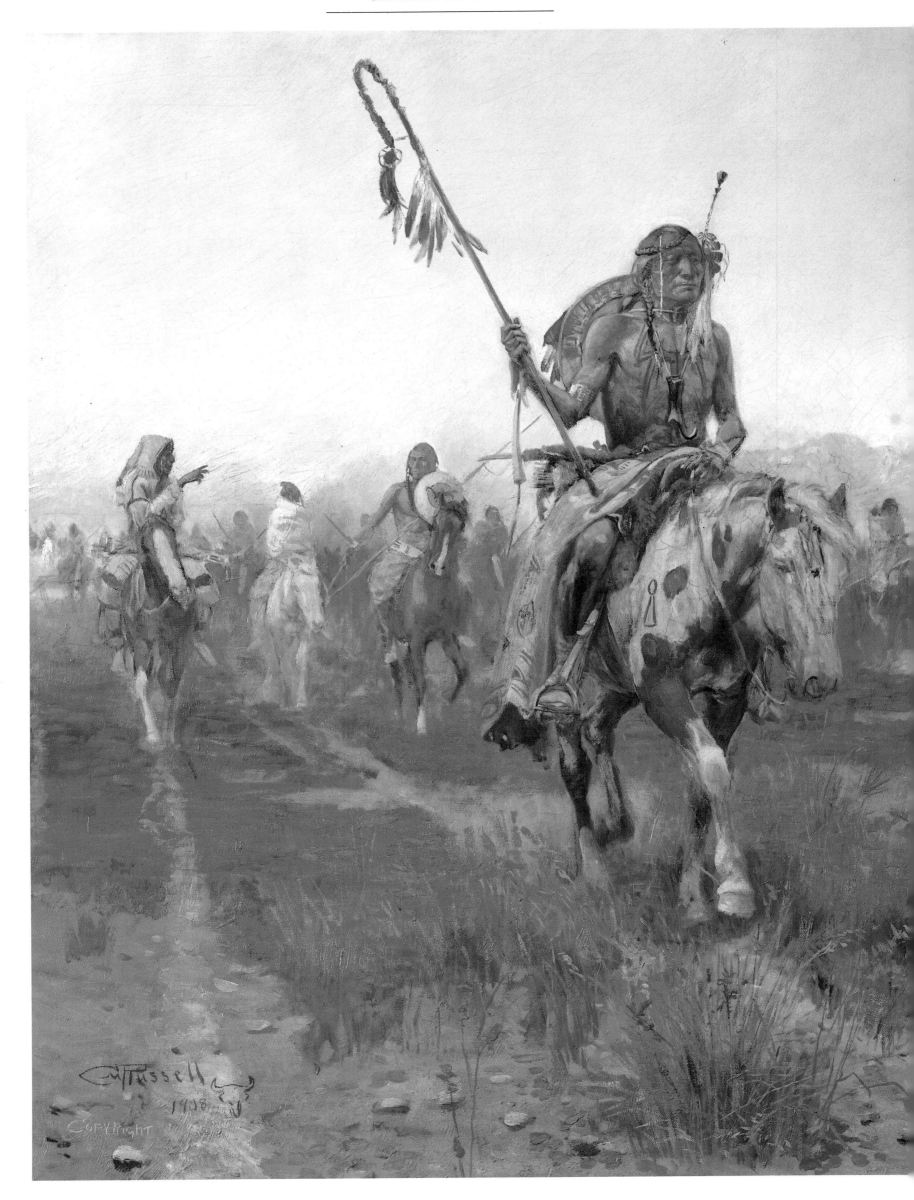

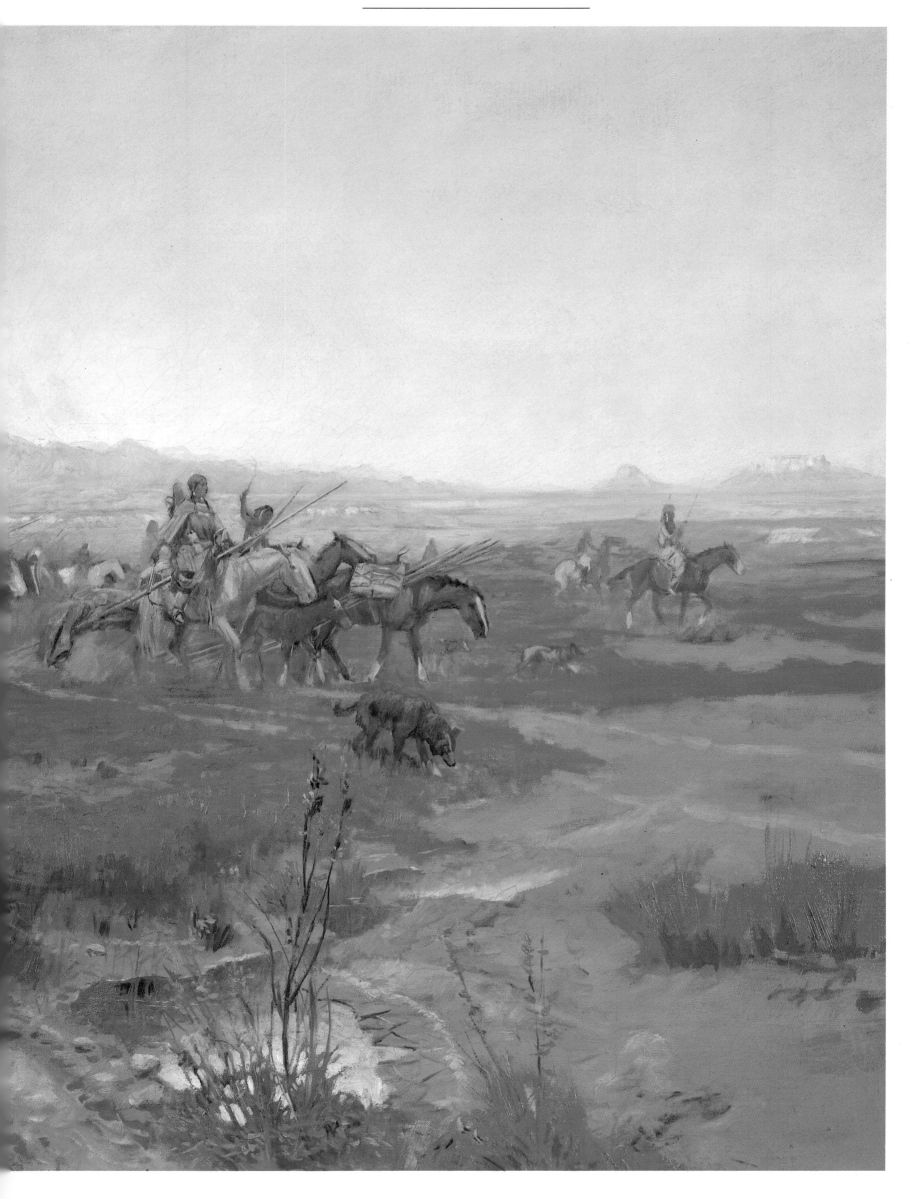

When Blackfeet and Sioux Meet
1908, oil on canvas, 20⅛×29⅞ in.
Sid Richardson Collection of Western Art, Fort Worth, TX

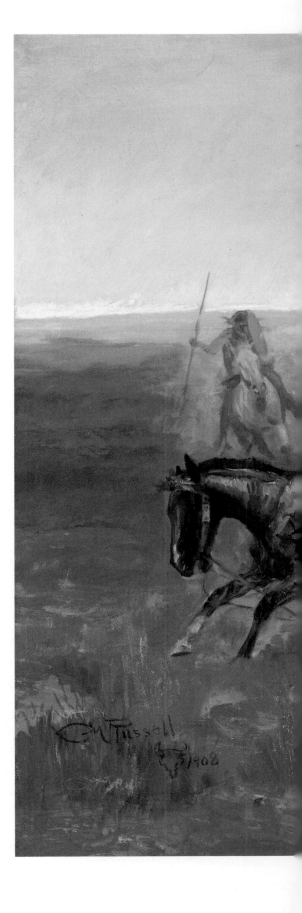

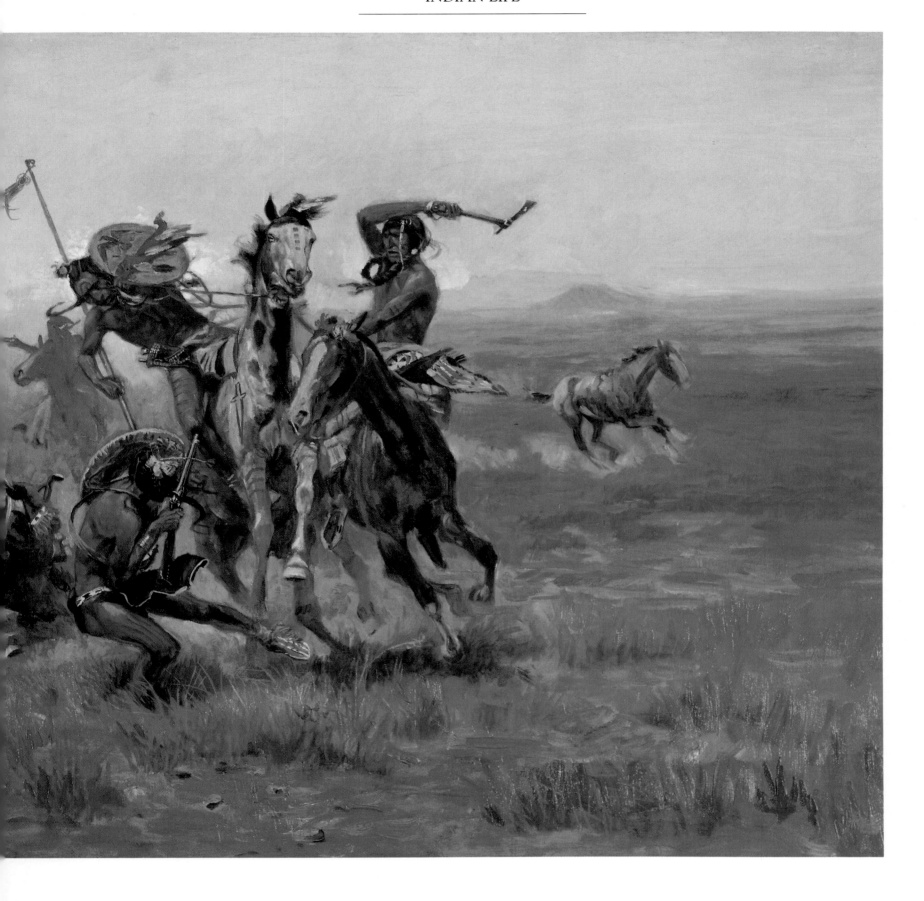

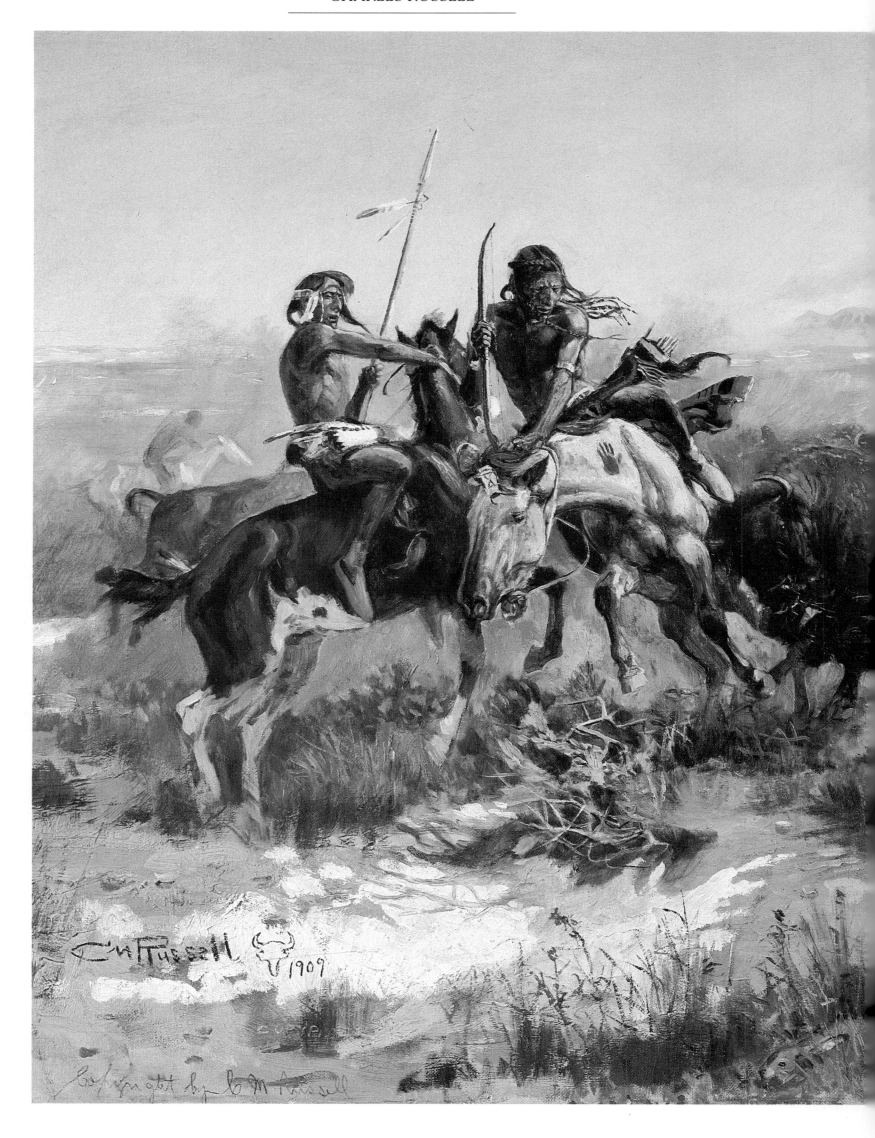

The Wounded Buffalo
1909, oil on canvas, 19⅞×30⅛ in.
Sid Richardson Collection of
Western Art, Fort Worth, TX

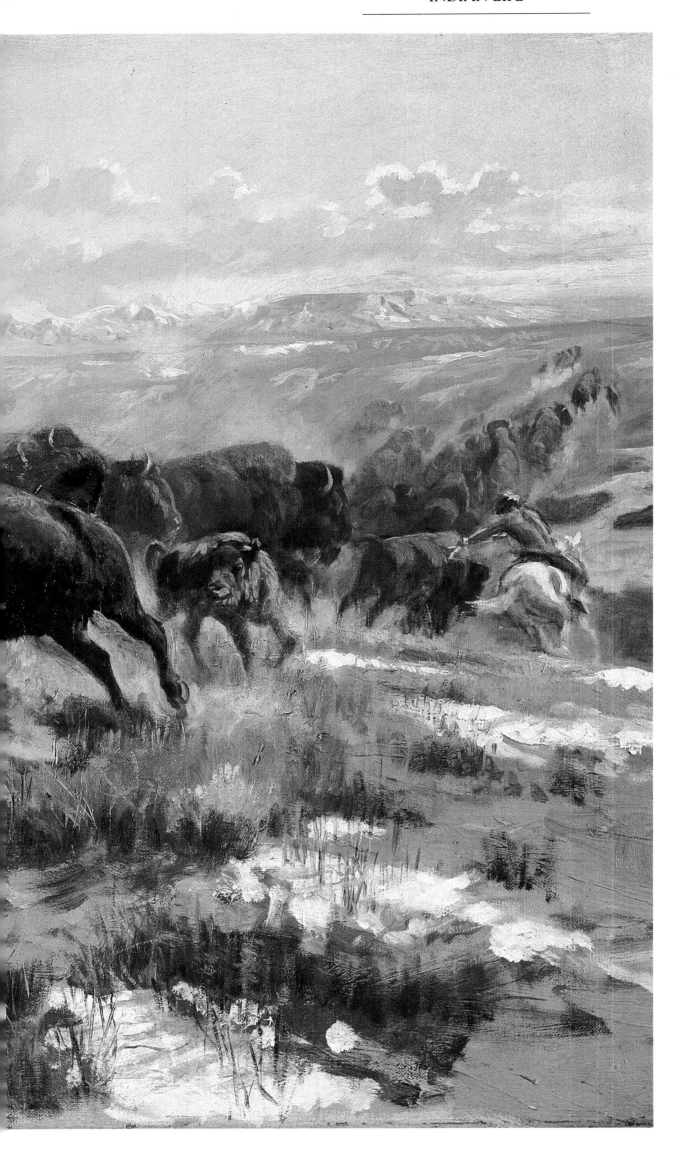

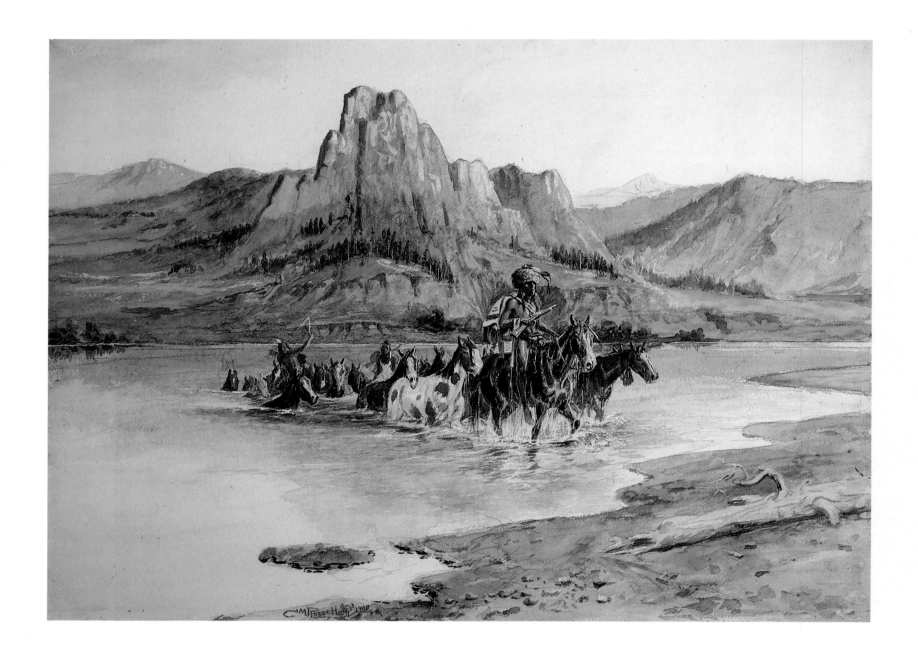

Pages 76-77:
The Ambush
n.d., oil on canvas, 25½×36½ in.
Bequest of Gertrude Mayn Backus, Montana Historical Society, Helena, MT

Return of the Horse Thieves
1900, watercolor, 21¼×29½ in.
C. M. Russell Museum, Great Falls, MT

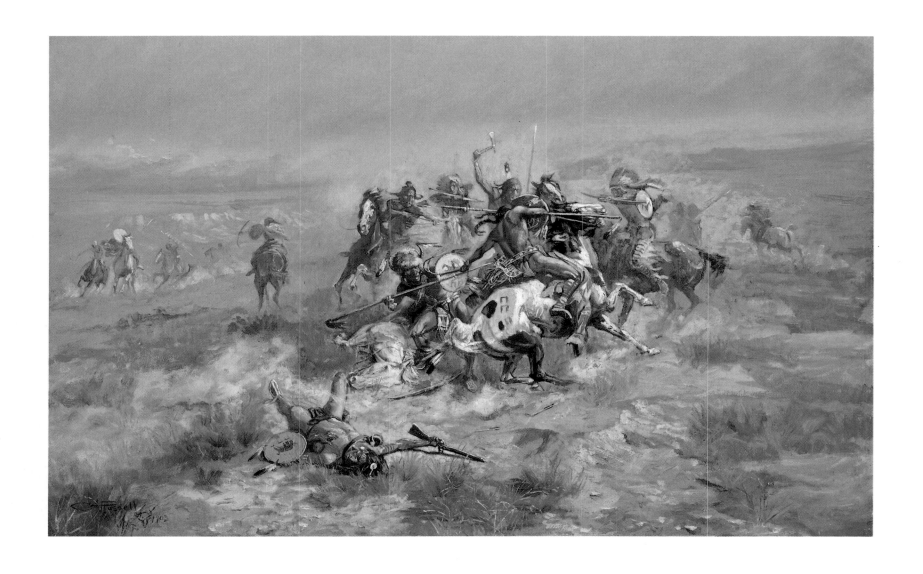

Counting Coup
1902, oil on canvas, 18⅛×30⅛ in.
Sid Richardson Collection of Western Art, Fort Worth, TX

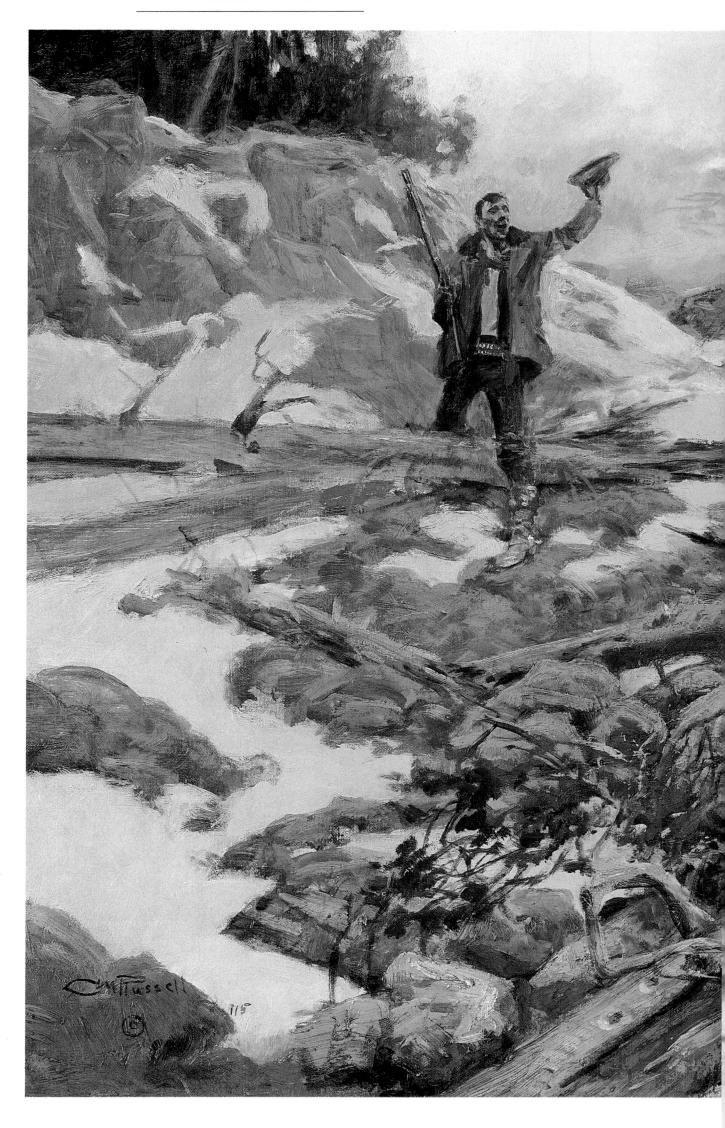

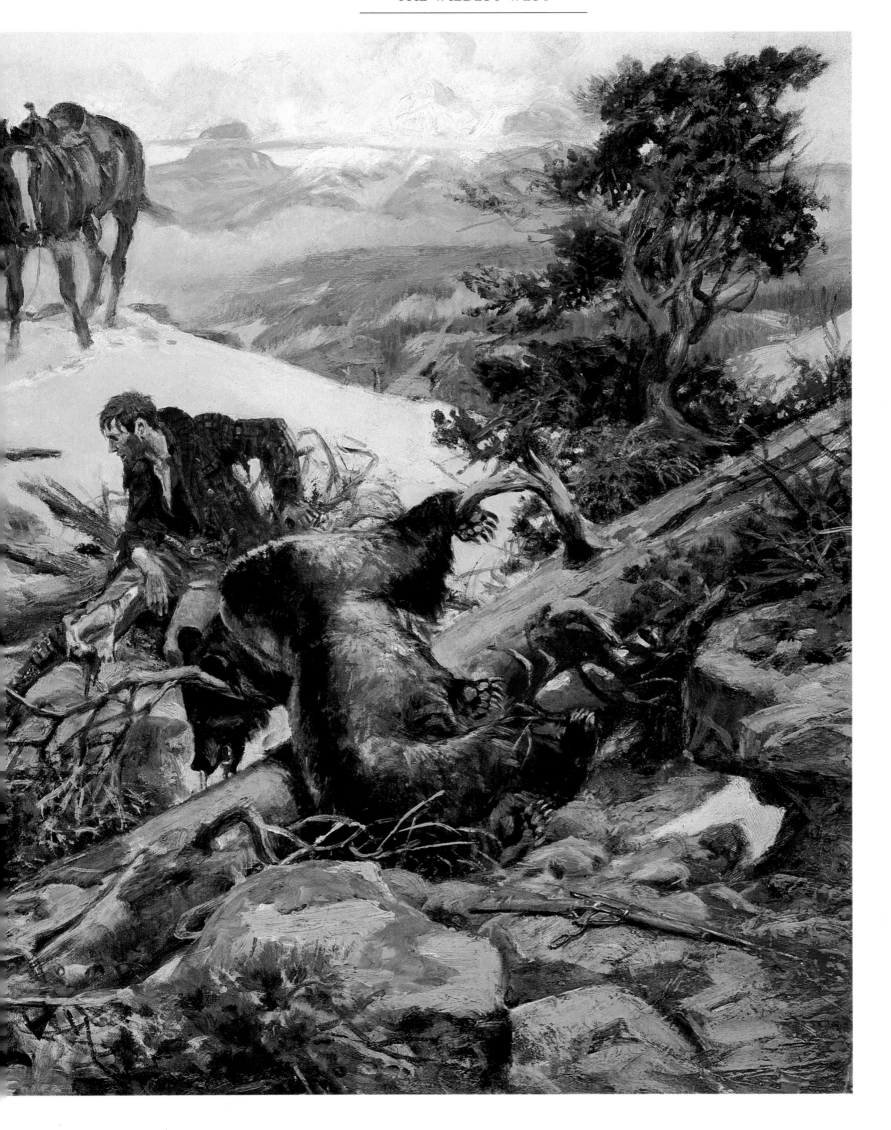

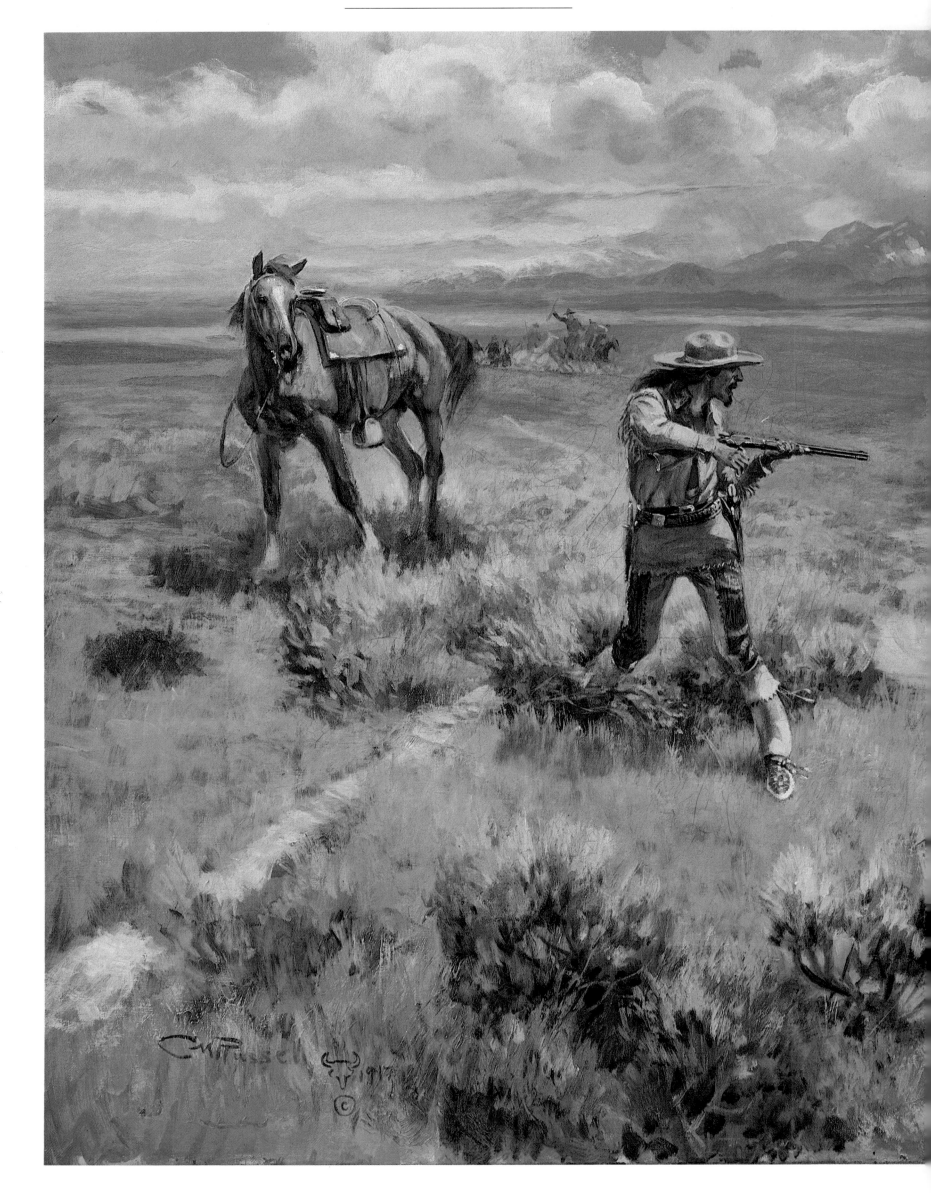

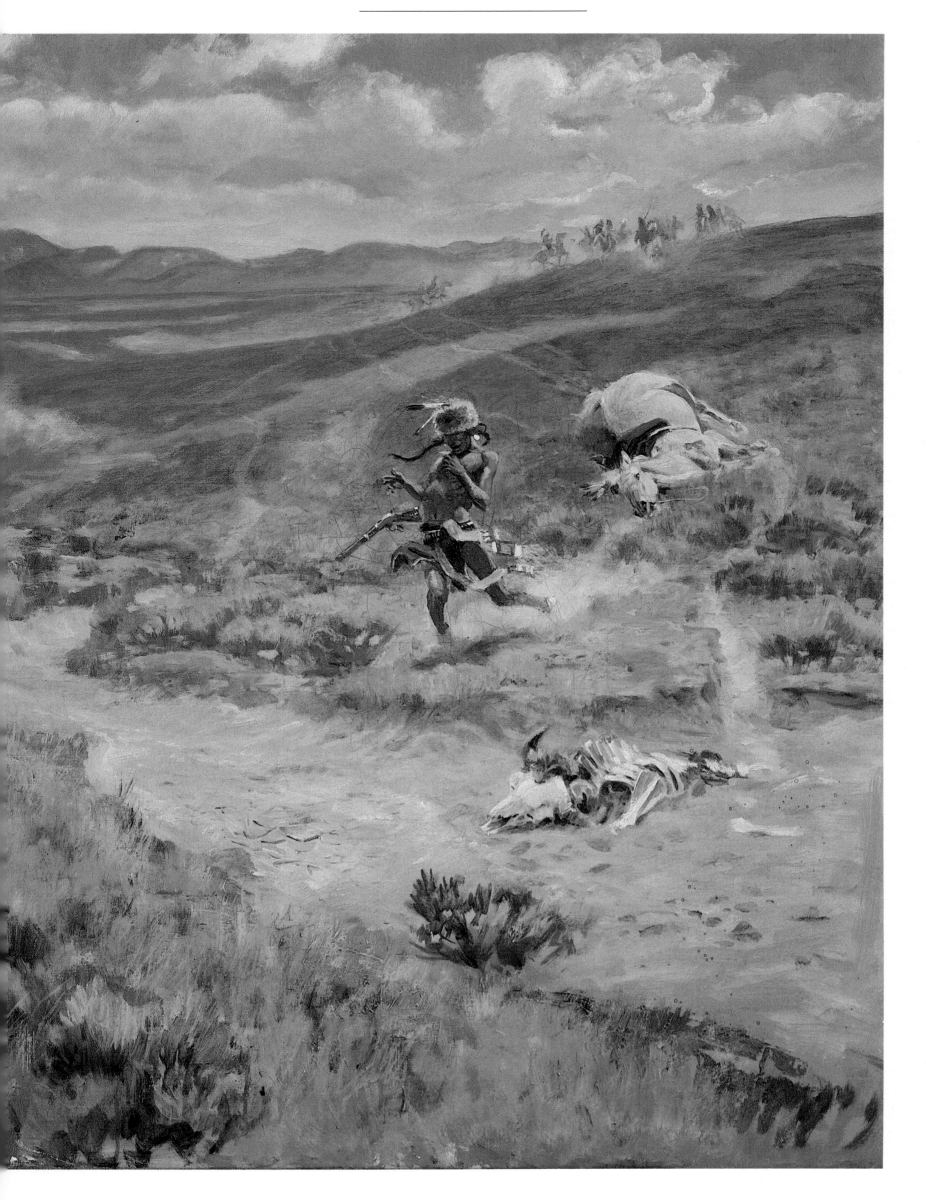

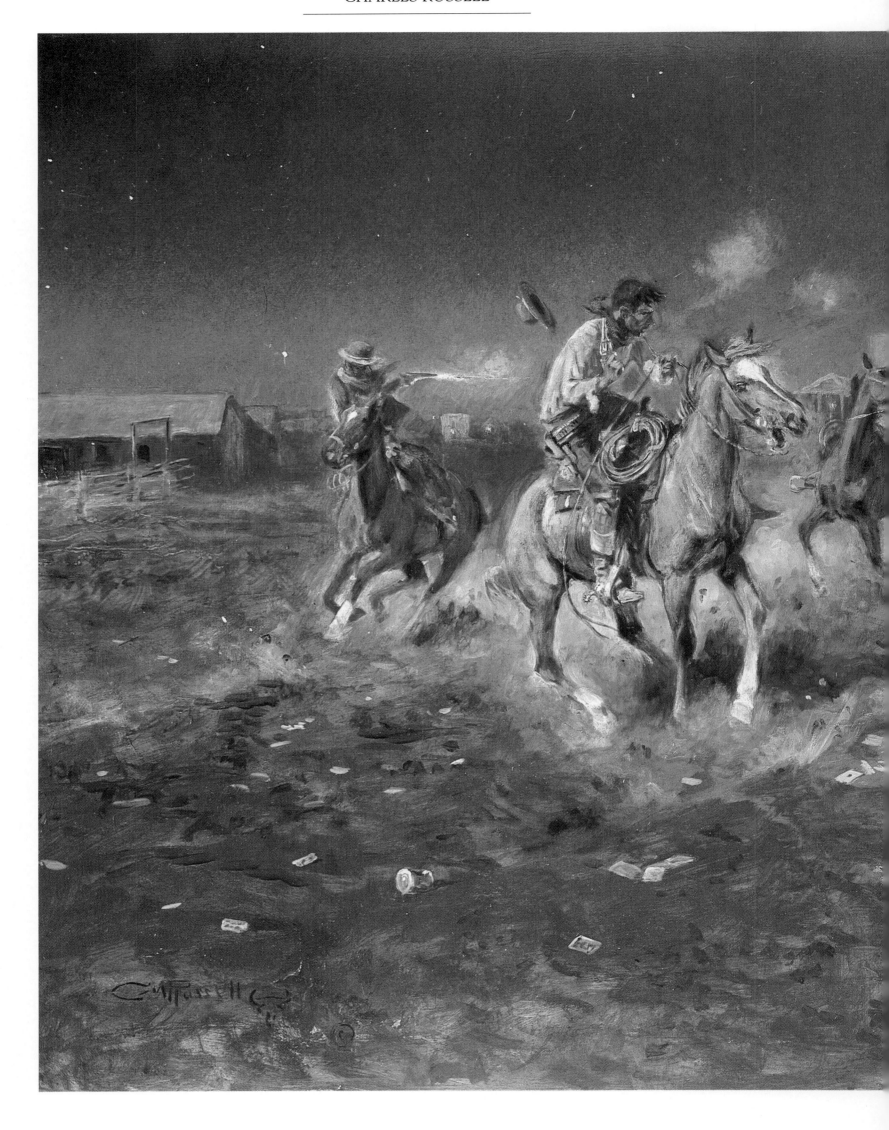

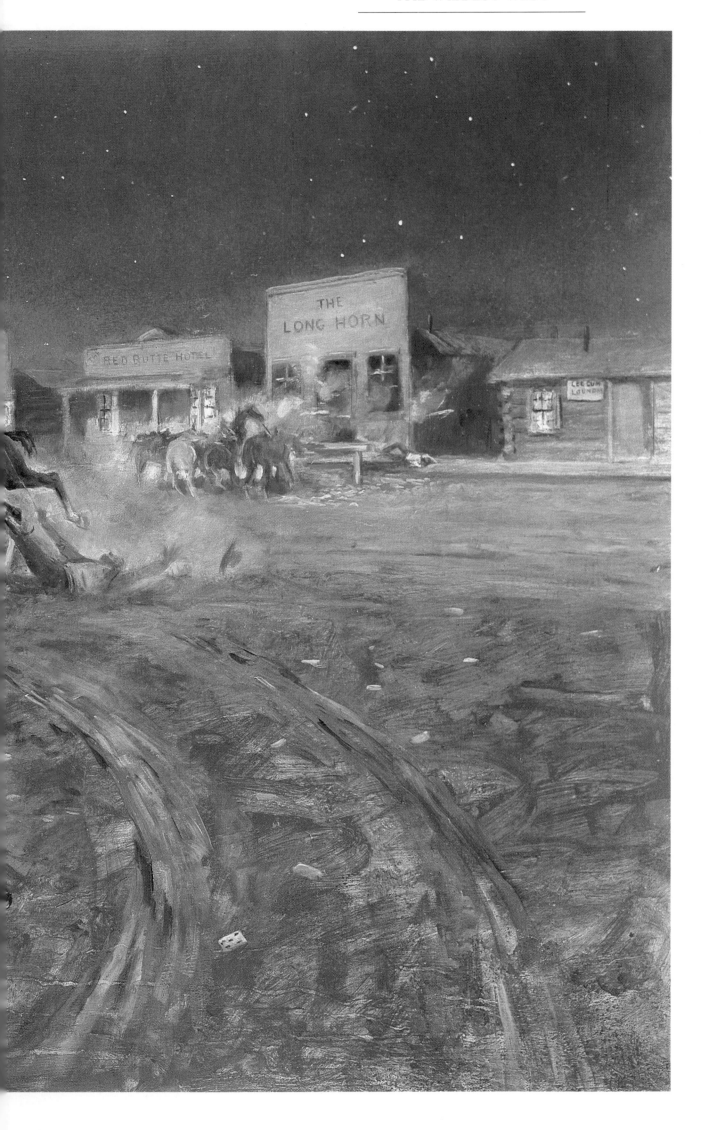

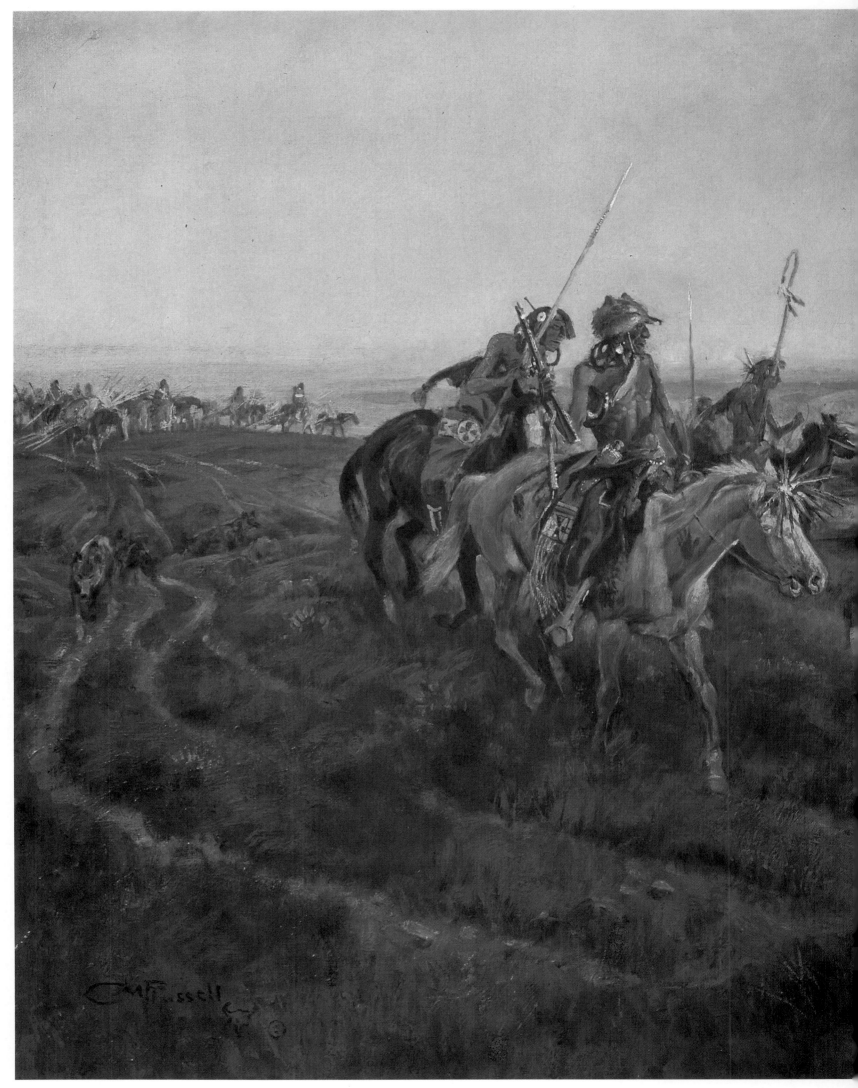

Pages 96-97:
When Guns Speak, Death Settles Dispute
n.d., oil on canvas, 24⅛×36⅛ in.
The Thomas Gilcrease Institute of American History and Art, Tulsa, OK

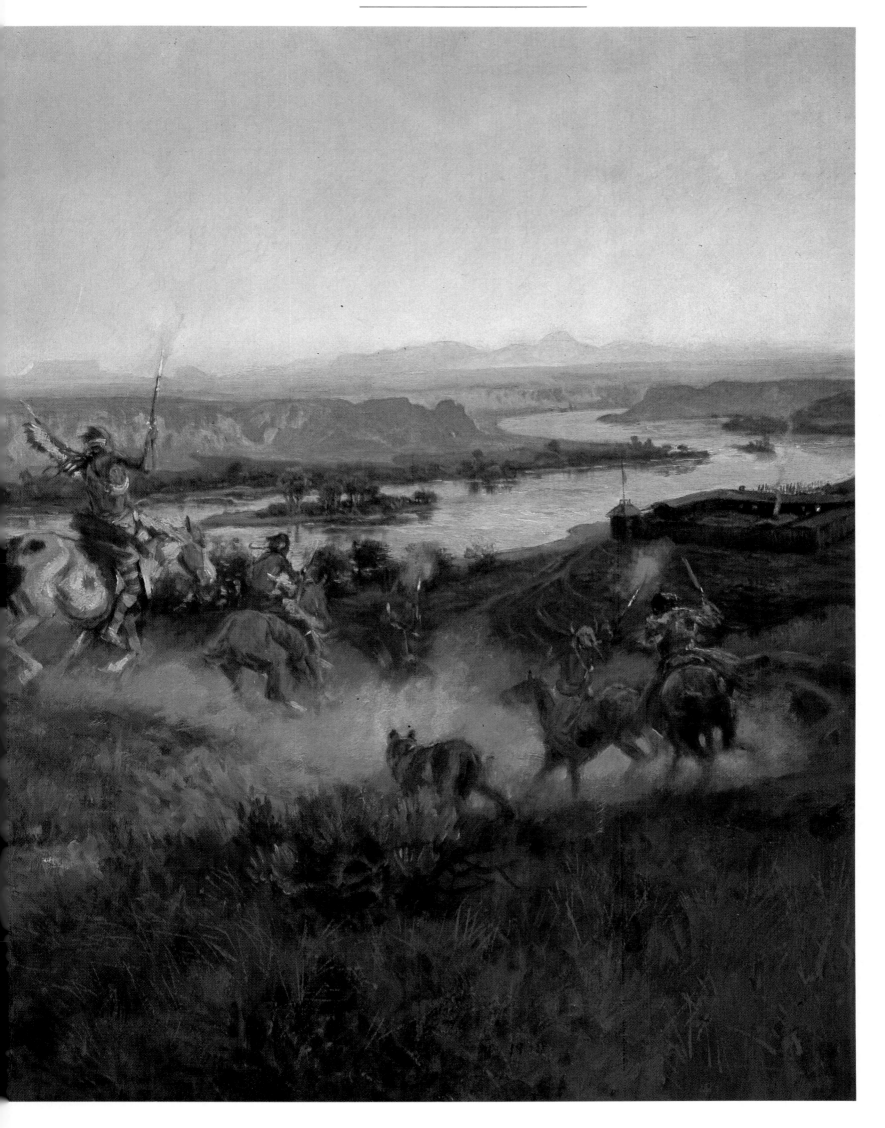

Salute to the Robe Trade
1920, oil on canvas, 29×47 in.
The Thomas Gilcrease Institute of American History and Art, Tulsa, OK

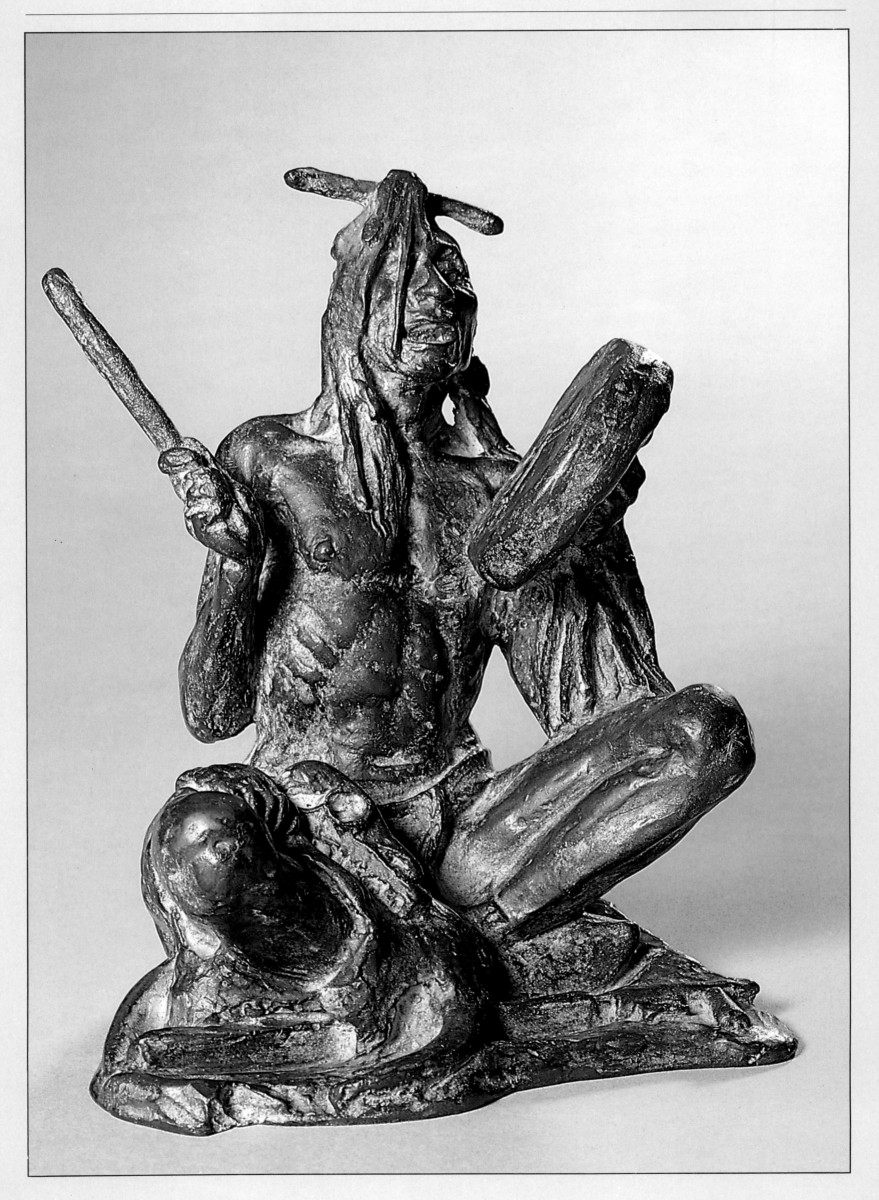

SCULPTURE

In his lifetime Charles Russell, who was considered by many to be the greatest living painter of western life, was barely known as a sculptor. Yet he excelled in this medium more than in any other. Russell produced a prodigious quantity of wax and clay models. Many of these were lost or destroyed – often by his own hand, as he would reuse the same wax of a model to form another. In total, 53 pieces of his sculpture models were cast in bronze during his lifetime, and many of the remaining original figures have been cast since.

Perhaps the very ease with which Russell modeled beeswax and clay caused him to underestimate sculpture as an art form. He rarely exhibited his sculptures, using them mainly as models for his paintings, or as gifts for friends. His close friends best appreciated Russell's facile modeling of almost anything that came to mind – wild animals, horses, and western characters of any dimension. These friends recount how in the middle of telling a story, Charlie would illustrate his point, much to his audience's delight, by suddenly producing a small wax model that he had fashioned behind his back or under the table.

Russell's knowledge and skill pertaining to three-dimensional form helped him to solve technical problems in painting. Russell imagined realistic western scenes of cowboys, Indians, buffalo, and his beloved horses in the round, as he had lived and experienced them. Often when he stumbled upon a question in painting – whether in regard to anatomy, light or movement – Charlie would make a wax model for reference. This points out why the figures of many a Russell sculpture replicate those in his paintings. For example in *Smoking Up*, his first sculpture cast in bronze, the image – that of a cowboy upon a rearing horse shooting a pistol – appears in such paintings as *Smokin' 'em Out*. One of his largest and most famous bronzes *Counting Coup*, depicting a group of Indians engaged in battle, parallels his equally impressive painting, *When Blackfeet and Sioux Meet*.

Frozen in time, Russell's sculptures capture myriad aspects of life in the West. He recorded the instinctive habits of wolves, bears, buffaloes – fighting, foraging or fleeing from hunters. Russell's passion for horses, combined with his years of intensive observation of their every movement, contributed to his sculpting some of the finest action scenes of equestrian figures. In such pieces as *Bucking Bronco* he caught men and horses in mid-action with feet off the ground as if he had clicked a camera. Russell also immortalized the spirit of the Indian through sculpture – whether he modeled them riding and hunting as in *Blackfoot War Chief* and *Buffalo Hunt*, or practicing their beliefs and rituals as in *The Medicine Man*.

The Medicine Man
c.1920, bronze, 7 in. high
Amon Carter Museum, Forth Worth, TX

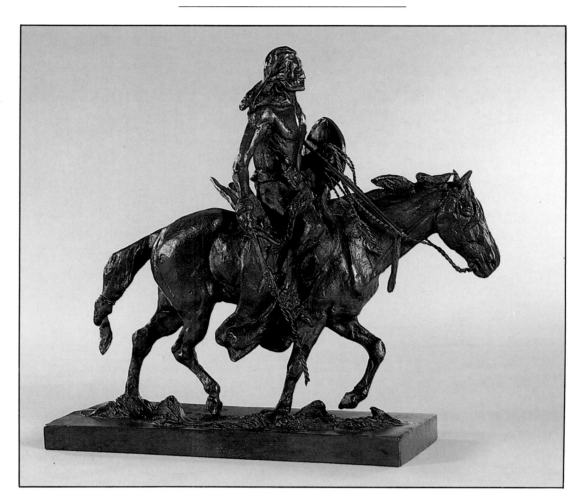

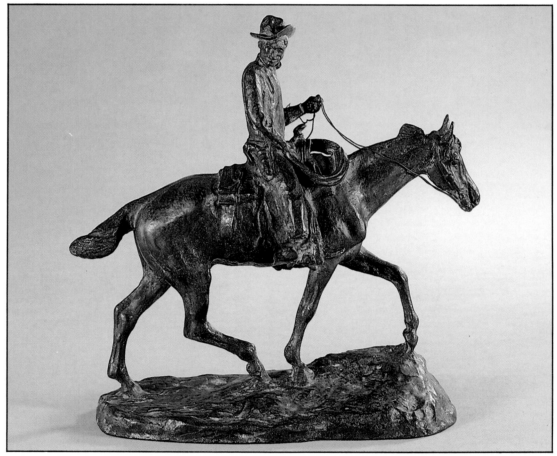

The Blackfoot War Chief
1900, bronze, 10⅝ in. high
Amon Carter Museum, Fort Worth, TX

Will Rogers
n.d., bronze, 11 in. high
Amon Carter Museum, Fort Worth, TX

Page 103:
Watcher of the Plains
n.d., bronze, 10¾×8¼ in.
The Buffalo Bill Historical Center, Cody, WY

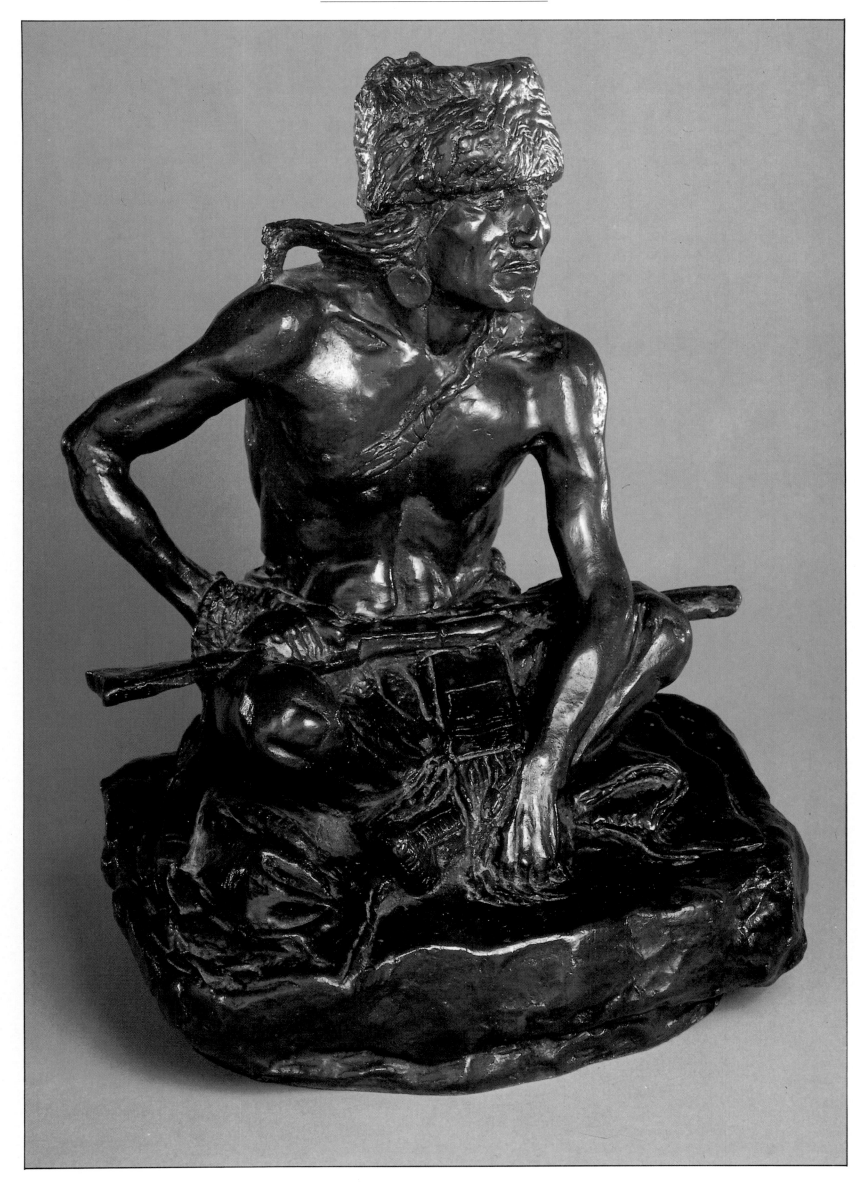

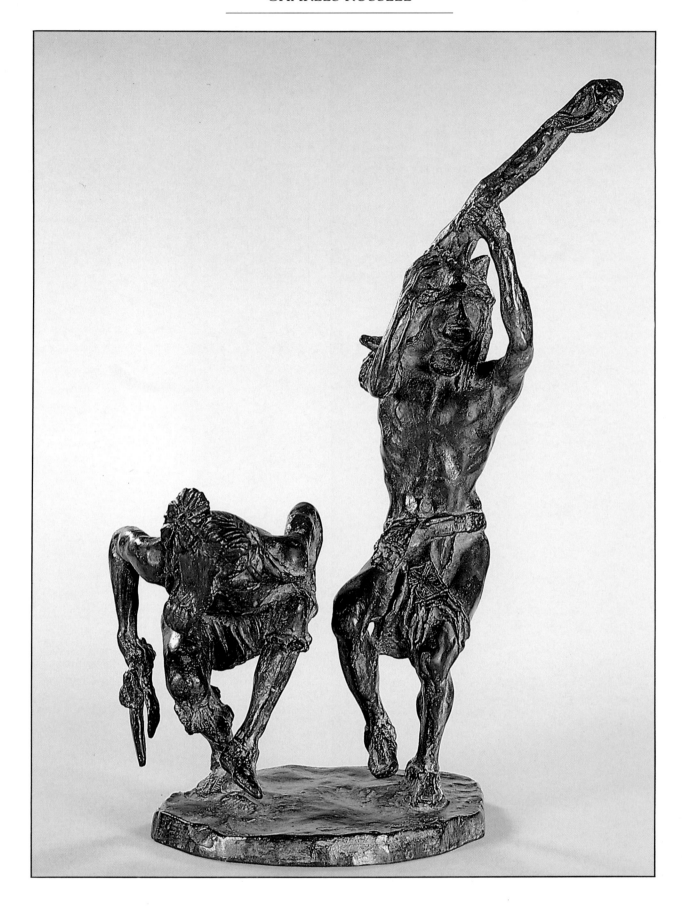

Page 105 (above):
Counting Coup
c.1904, bronze, 11¼ in. high
Amon Carter Museum, Fort Worth, TX

Page 105 (below):
Buffalo Hunt
c.1905, bronze, 10 in. high
Amon Carter Museum, Fort Worth, TX

The Scalp Dance (The Blackfoot War Dance)
c.1904, bronze, 13½ in. high
Amon Carter Museum, Fort Worth, TX

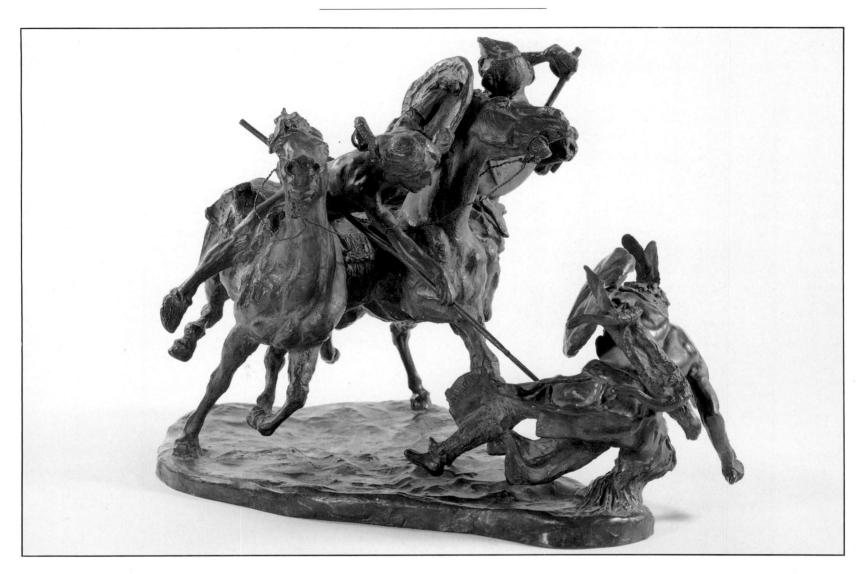

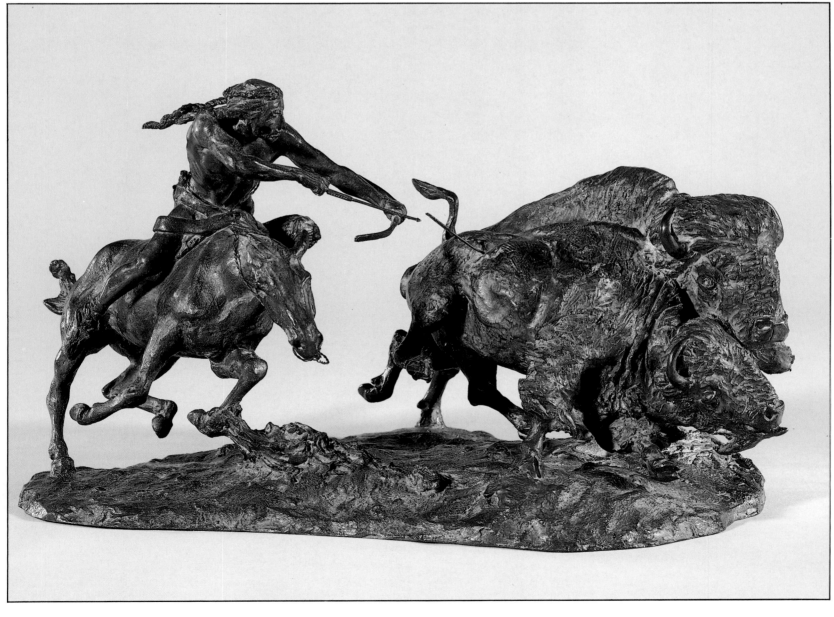

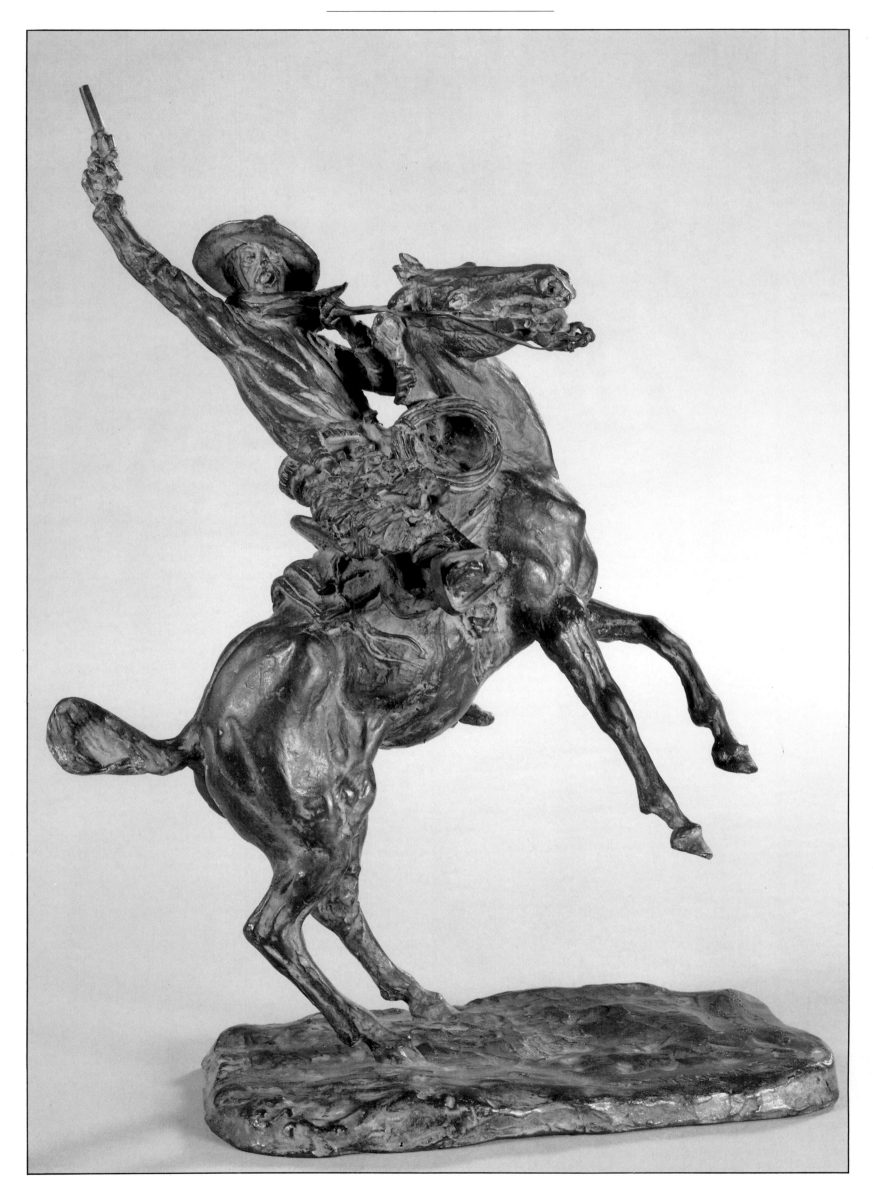

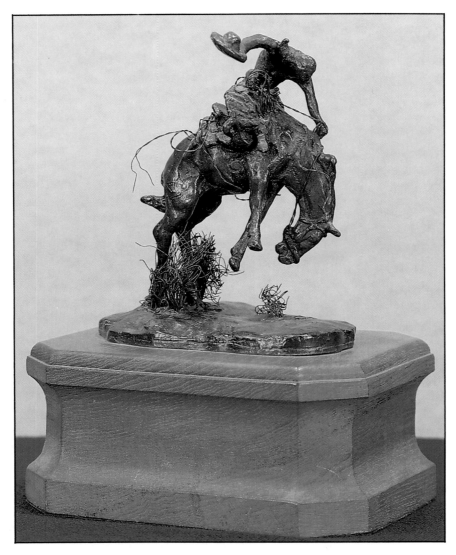

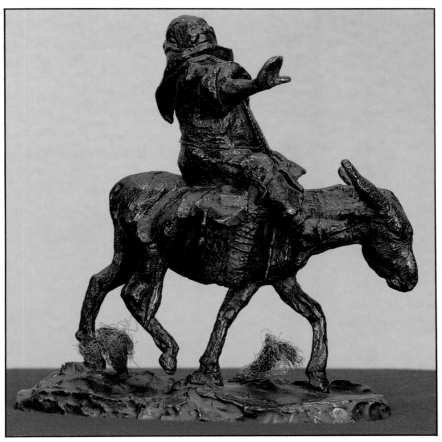

Page 106:
Smoking Up
c.1904, bronze, 12¾ in. high
Amon Carter Museum, Fort Worth, TX

Bucking Bronco
1905, bronze, 5¾×4¼×3 in.
C. M. Russell Museum, Great Falls, MT

Friar Tuck
c.1910, bronze, 7½×7½×3½ in.
C. M. Russell Museum, Great Falls, MT

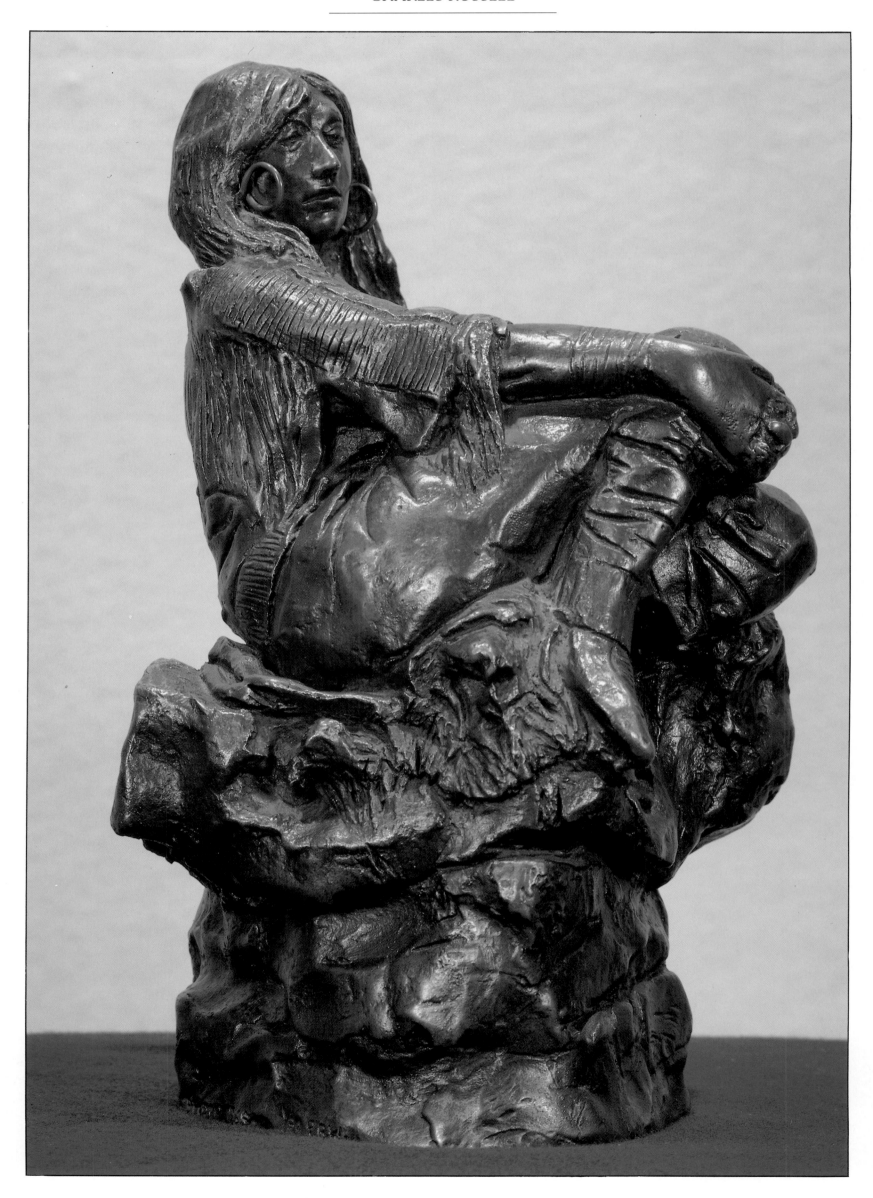

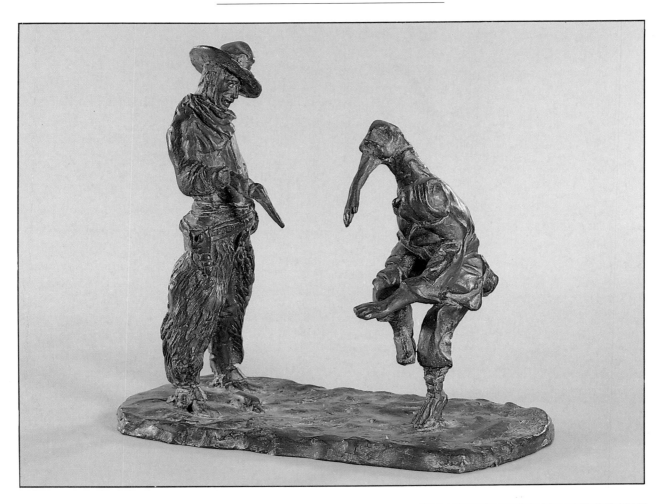

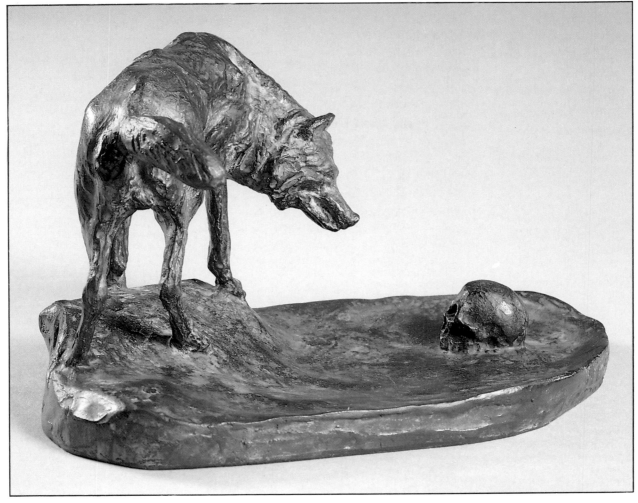

Page 108:
Piegan Maiden
c.1910, bronze, 10¼ × 5¼ × 6¼ in.
C. M. Russell Museum, Great Falls, MT

Painting the Town
n.d., bronze, 11 in. high
Amon Carter Museum, Fort Worth, TX

The Last Laugh
1916, bronze, 4⅜ in. high
Amon Carter Museum, Fort Worth, TX

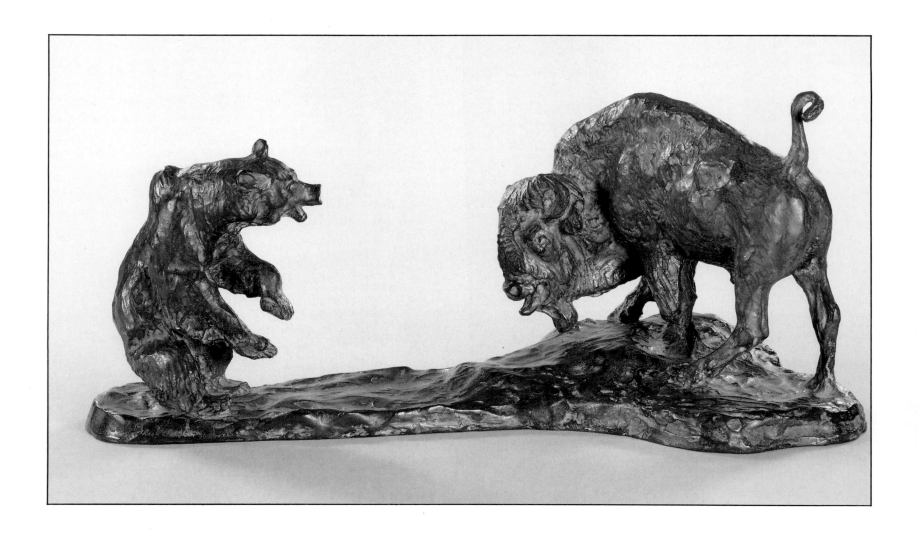

The Bluffers
c.1924, bronze, 7½ in. high
Amon Carter Museum, Fort Worth, TX

Page 111:
Jim Bridger
1925, bronze, 14¼ in. high
The Buffalo Bill Historical Center, Cody, WY

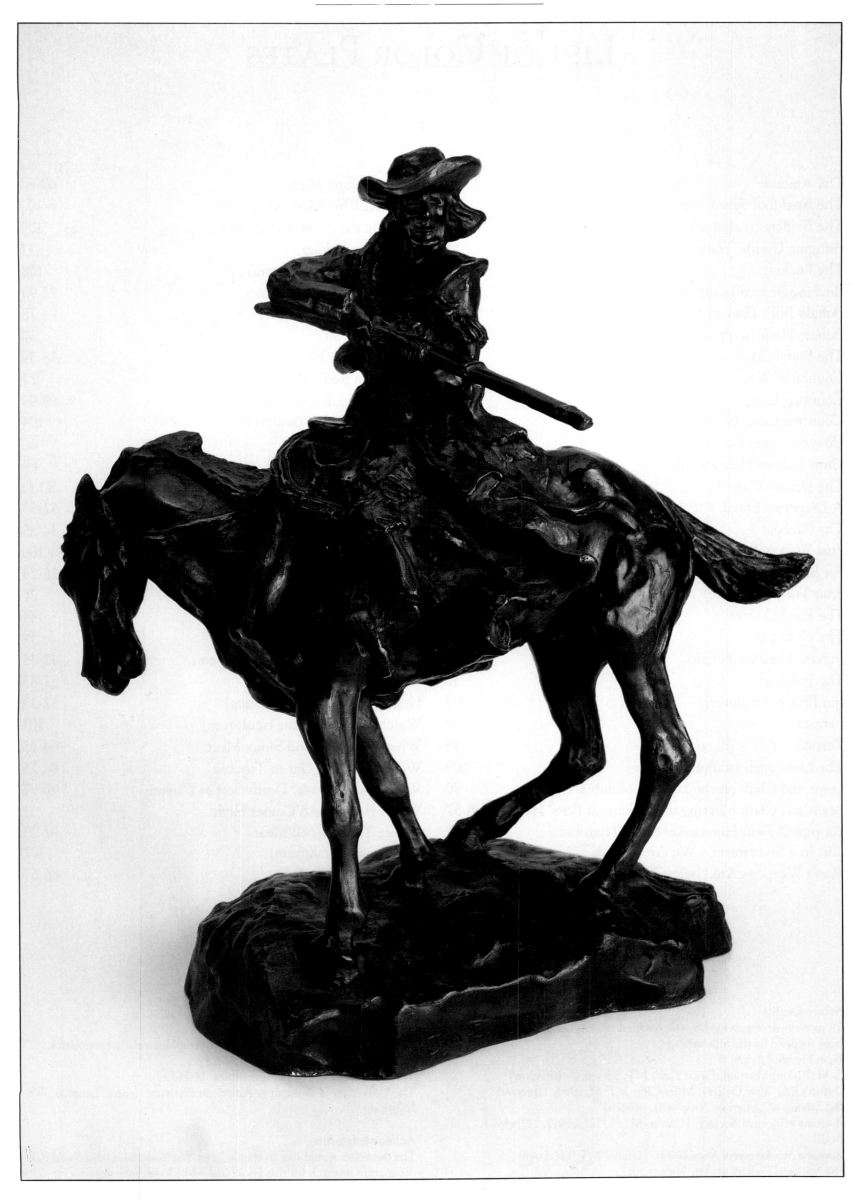